RISE

RISE

HOW JEREMY CORBYN
INSPIRED THE YOUNG TO CREATE
A NEW SOCIALISM

LIAM YOUNG

**SIMON &
SCHUSTER**

London · New York · Sydney · Toronto · New Delhi

A CBS COMPANY

First published in Great Britain by Simon & Schuster UK Ltd, 2018
A CBS COMPANY

1 3 5 7 9 10 8 6 4 2

Simon & Schuster UK Ltd
1st Floor
222 Gray's Inn Road
London WC1X 8HB

www.simonandschuster.co.uk

Simon & Schuster Australia, Sydney
Simon & Schuster India, New Delhi

A CIP catalogue record for this book
is available from the British Library.

ISBN: 978-1-4711-7134-5
Ebook ISBN: 978-1-4711-7135-2

Typeset in Bembo by M Rules
Printed and bound by CPI Group (UK) Ltd, Croydon, CR0 4YY

Simon & Schuster UK Ltd are committed to sourcing paper
that is made from wood grown in sustainable forests and support the Forest
Stewardship Council, the leading international forest certification organisation.
Our books displaying the FSC logo are printed on FSC certified paper.

CONTENTS

For my family and all those who kept me grounded while making all of this possible.

For the future.

Introduction

A Strange Beginning

'So, what do you want to do when you're older?' asked the prime minister. 'Well, I want your job,' I shot back. Aged only nine, I had somehow managed to find myself attempting to usurp Tony Blair from office in the final days of his administration.

I later discovered that forty years prior to this moment, a young Bill Clinton was snapped in a similar scenario during a meeting with President Kennedy in the White House Rose Garden. Though my political ambition at the time was no more developed than having a quixotic desire to end world hunger, as with Clinton, a handshake inspired me to pursue a career in politics. I often wonder if Blair – the man who stood me in front of him for a photograph after he said he would need it just in case I ever did become prime minister – has ever seen any of the numerous interviews I have given, berating him as a figure of a bygone era. I doubt he has, but I am sure that he may regret what he started when he wished me 'the best of luck' with my ambition.

My interest in politics from this young age has always been the cause of some fascination to the people who were aware of it. From the primary school teachers who would scribble 'remember me when you are prime minister!' at the end of my annual school reports, to the senior politicians to whom I would write on a regular basis, there has always been a baffled air of ignorance surrounding the political engagement and opinions of young people – despite the goodwill and encouragement of those I have mentioned. For so long, politics has been an area of life that – as far as the adult world was concerned – we young people did not really belong in.

But, within my own family, my ardent interest in politics was viewed simply as second nature. I remember my mum preparing a den for me when I was eight years old, so that I could pull an all-nighter as the 2005 general election results rolled in and the Labour Party was returned to power for a historic and record-breaking third term. I was even allowed to have the next day off from school to 'recover' – 'bunking off' never came into it.

My parents were not particularly interested in politics themselves. My mum and dad met when they were both at school and their first child, my eldest sister Demi, was stillborn when my mum was just sixteen. Until they separated a few years ago, we were a typical working-class family with our own share of joys and struggles. My dad was a plumber and my mum had worked in a range of jobs, from a make-up desk in Debenhams to an events organiser who worked with the likes of the Sugababes and Status Quo. Our familial engagement with politics was practically nil. My dad detested politicians, the political system and everything that he believed it stood for. My mum voted more out of a loyalty to the Labour Party than any real passion for the positions that the party espoused.

However, I would be lying if I said it was the handshake of the formidable Tony Blair that ignited the inspiration for my political ambition. Instead, it was an even more towering figure – despite standing more than half a foot shorter than me these days – that first piqued my interest in the world of politics. Though I was not around at the time that my grandparents – Roland and Linda Hurst – were active in our local Labour Party, the stories I have been told of my granddad's leadership of the city council helped to shape my early understanding of politics.

When he lent me his recording of the 1997 general election coverage, I was gripped. Their tales of how they had danced until the early hours of the morning at Lincoln's Labour Club (Grafton House), as they believed Labour's landslide would enable them to change the world, inspired me. I recall watching the Portillo moment and the point at which Tony Blair declared his 'new dawn' to a crowd of thousands. I remember waking up, after momentarily falling asleep, to the sight of Blair's limousine travelling back from the palace to begin the work of government. Though just a year old when all of this happened, and eight at the time of watching it, I have always felt like I was there. My gran often told me that when my granddad was elected to Lincoln City Council, he was motivated by a belief that he 'would change the world'. My interest in politics came from this very simple fact; I remember thinking: *That's exactly what I want to do.*

Like my grandparents, I have always believed that politics exists as an arena for change – it is a vocation where the desire for change can actually be put into practice. It was not a passion for politics that brought me to believe in this, but rather a passion for change that brought me to politics. I always winced at the criticism that such a view was naïve, that all politicians were the same and that politics seldom changed anything.

Despite what some say, I believe that politics has never been a distant concept for people my age. I was not born into a political dynasty or forced into a particular party. Most of my political beliefs were formed while working for £3.50 an hour at Sports Direct on a zero-hours contract as I tried to complete my A-Levels. Dealing with the humiliation of being practically strip-searched upon leaving work every evening is a sad reality for many working-class young people trapped in uncertain and precarious employment. Though some on the right believe that the young will abandon their socialism once in the workplace, it was this experience that enthused a spirit of radicalism within me.

My views have also been shaped by the accumulation of £54,000 worth of tuition fee and maintenance debt for having the audacity to pursue a university education. They have been formed by the conversations I have had with those struggling to get by, with nurses forced to use food banks and with those who, in 2017, are forced to sleep rough on the streets of our country. These are events and conversations that many of us engage with at some point in our lives – if our eyes are open. In this sense, politics remains an essential part of all of us, regardless of age.

Yet until the leadership election that saw Jeremy Corbyn take charge of the Labour Party in September 2015, we had seen very little interest shown in the views of young people, and that remained true for much of the period that followed up until the 2017 general election. Rather than being interested in where the Labour leader's support comes from, or why his appeal has extended well beyond the typical Labour Party member, it has been easier for an establishment clique to laugh. As Janan Ganesh of the *Financial Times* so elegantly put it: 'You can do an analysis of Corbyn and his "movement" (I have done it) but the essence of the whole thing is that they are just thick as pigshit.'

But while the establishment mocked, I have watched and participated in this phenomenon with a keen interest that has gone beyond partisan belief. At the time of Corbyn's first leadership victory, I was nineteen years old. I was about to begin my second year at the London School of Economics. Little did I know that I would also be embarking on a political journey of my own, regularly contributing at the *Independent* and the *New Statesman* as one of the few pro-Corbyn commentators. Though decried as 'Corbyn's fanboy' and a number of other adoring names, my belief then and now that he would broaden Labour's appeal has been proven correct. Rather than the product of misguided idolatry or hero worship, as my critics painted it, my belief in Corbyn came from my being rooted in the class and community of which I am proud.

WHY RISE?

Whether it be the Tory Party inflicting the pain of a series of austerity measures on the backs of the young, or Labour's deputy leader, Tom Watson, suggesting in 2016 that our 'young arms' were being twisted by 'old hands', there is still a failure to understand why people of my generation support Jeremy Corbyn's vision in such large numbers. It is the central task of this book to shed some light on that very question – to explore exactly what this appeal is and to assess whether it will endure.

However, there will be no attempt to define 'Corbynism', as some seem so obsessed with doing. The truth is that to do so misses the entire point of Corbyn's appeal among the young. You could call Corbynism a social movement of its own making. It clearly stands as a direct opponent to neoliberalism and to austerity, to war and to violence, but Corbynism is something much bigger than the set of beliefs that Jeremy Corbyn supports. Indeed, I want to dispel the myth that young people are part of some cult that worships at the altar of Corbyn alone. Those I have spoken to while researching this book wholeheartedly refute this myth. Luke Atkins, a 19-year-old student, calls this attitude a 'media invention', while Rhys Warriner, a 21-year-old, believes Corbynism to be nothing more than 'common-sense politics powered by social justice'. One young activist, who didn't want to be named but who spent hours every day on the doorstep, told me that they 'didn't care about the labels'.

There is a common thread of understanding that chimes with my own reaction to Corbyn's platform. Labour's offer at the last election, that things don't have to stay the same and that it is possible to change the whole way our country is run, had the ability to command the attention of those who are most optimistic. It is, therefore, somewhat unsurprising that the most optimistic generation bought into an optimistic vision for the future in unprecedented numbers. Though some (incorrectly) label Corbyn as a dogmatic Marxist or Trotskyite, the truth is that his platform is unique. It is why Jeremy Corbyn remains central to this story while also being somewhat removed from it – it isn't that young people have flocked to the Labour leader because he is who he is, it is that he was prepared to say something different and offer radical solutions to current problems. It is socialism, but not as we have known it. Simon Fletcher, Corbyn's former campaign director, has perfectly called this the 'new socialism'.

It is this new socialism that will be defined across the pages of this book. For me and my generation, the new socialism develops the traditional aims of the socialist cause for a modern technological age. Born of the financial crisis of the early 21st century and the prevailing decade of stagnation that followed, this new ideology is centred on young people's value-driven desires to change the world for the better – through collective solidarity, respect and equality. Corbyn has inspired and fostered a youthful optimism that a better world is indeed possible.

Within that new socialism is an abandonment of the old and tired ways of establishment politics. What has been born in its place is what Branwen Cleaver, a 19-year-old student, describes as 'the ability to enthuse millions of young people, and politically frustrated older generations alike'. In analysing the election campaign and what has happened before and since, we can reveal just how it was that young people have come to support Corbyn, and the politics he represents. This stands in contrast to the previous failure of politicians to engage with the young and our ambitions for the future.

In keeping with the new socialism, this book will not be all about me. It won't be all about Jeremy Corbyn or his inner circle either. There will not be undue concentration on, or fascination with, the internal squabbles of the Labour Party campaign and its progress outside the election. Instead, it will focus on how young people like me got excited by Corbyn's promise and what is yet to come – on the contribution of the young to the beginning of a movement that is only just gathering momentum.

When I started writing this book, I reached out to young people across the country of all different political persuasions by asking them to reply to questions that I had posted online as well as meeting with some people in the flesh. It is true that most of those who got back to me were Labour supporters. Given how many young people backed the Labour Party at the 2017 general election, this is somewhat unsurprising. I asked many questions, both online and offline. I wanted this story to be informed by the very voices that made it happen. Online, I had over 4,000 email responses, of which 500 were selected for raising pertinent points that will be discussed throughout this book. All questions were asked loosely, focusing on the idea of a 21st-century form of socialism. I wanted to know why other young people got involved, how deep this involvement was and whether these young people will continue to be involved.

There will be plenty of names in this book that you will almost certainly not recognise – as with some already quoted above – because you are not supposed to recognise them. But they are the names that matter. They are the names of the people inspired by this new movement, the names of our future. *Rise* is much more than words on paper. It is an attempt to abandon the patronising ways of the old politics and replace it with a politics that puts the voices of young people at its very heart.

PART ONE

Rising Up

Chapter 1

THE TIRED ESTABLISHMENT

AN UNLIKELY RISE

'The media and many of us simply didn't understand the views of young people in our country. They were turned off by the way politics was being conducted. We have to and must change that. The fightback gathers speed and gathers pace.'

These were the words of Labour Party leader Jeremy Corbyn during his first leadership victory speech on 12 September 2015. I was there to hear them. And never did the words of a politician ring so true to a 19-year-old who was not just interested in politics, but also sick of the way that it was being done. Having volunteered on Jeremy's leadership campaign, I had a ticket for the 2015 leadership conference, but I was broke. I used the last £50 in my bank account and travelled to London from Lincoln to see whether what I had hoped could be possible would actually happen.

I sat in the crowd and told those around me that I couldn't

allow myself to believe that they would let him win. I had a burning feeling that every single part of the establishment would be used against him and I honestly doubted the impartiality of the whole system. This was, of course, ludicrous, but so strong was my belief that Corbyn could change everything for ever that I couldn't help but entertain such a conspiracy theory. Little did I know that, three floors above me in the Queen Elizabeth II Conference Centre, Jeremy Corbyn and his campaign chief John McDonnell had already been made aware of the thumping victory over half an hour earlier.

When the result was announced, it was clear to me that this was the first of many triumphs to come for my generation. It was, after all, a victory that had been largely powered by young people – whether it was the hundreds of youthful and enthusiastic voices that campaigned in the leadership election or the new recruits that joined the party, Corbyn had marked his card with the young at this early stage. The plan to engage with them was a clear intention from the outset. He had developed a specific policy paper on young people that was 'compiled in discussion with more than 1,000 Young Labour supporters from across Britain ... enabling them to have a say in the design of their own futures'. Such a statement was far more than rhetoric. It is this idea of 'enabling' that rests at the core of his appeal to my generation. He never spoke at us. We never had things decided for us. For the first time in decades, we were *asked*. And we responded. Having been patronised for years, we answered the call to forge our own future.

Weeks before the result, I can remember walking down

Oxford Street in London with a group of friends frantically refreshing my Twitter feed as the deadline for nominations in the upcoming Labour leadership election approached. It is important to recall that Corbyn had put himself forward as a candidate in the Labour leadership race less than a fortnight before and that, prior to the announcement of his candidacy, the left found itself in a pit of despair because the other candidates all came from the right or centre of the party, and they feared that another opportunity would be lost after Ed Miliband's defeat in the 2015 general election. In order to be able to run, he needed the support of thirty-five MPs, and many in Parliament were highly sceptical about him.

Just a few weeks prior to the moment that McDonnell would successfully ensure Corbyn's place on the ballot, he had written in an article for *Labour Briefing* that the current period was the 'darkest hour that socialists in Britain have faced since the Attlee government fell in 1951'. Little did he know that, moments after midday on 15 June 2015, he would announce the beginning of our brightest hour, tweeting from his account: 'As Jeremy's agent I can confirm that he is on the Labour leadership ballot with 35 nominations. Thank you everyone.' What some initially saw as nothing more than a chance to open a debate soon became the beginning of a new political movement that would defy expectations and successfully challenge the fundamental nature of British politics.

If politics seems to have changed suddenly since that day in 2015, then that is because it has. Just 637 days separate the day Jeremy Corbyn was first elected leader of the Labour

Party and the morning that the shock of Labour's comeback in the 2017 general election became clear. Within that time, much has happened. Out of those 637 days, there was a total of three weeks during which the establishment took seriously the prospect of him becoming prime minister – or even doing better than expected.

Despite reforming Prime Minister's Questions to the People's Question Time, forcing U-turns on tax credits, police cuts, Saudi prisons and other issues within Parliament, the Labour Party was taken seriously for only twenty-one days. Despite boosting party membership to levels not seen in decades at a time when party membership continues to decline across the globe, with European socialists wondering what on earth was going on, the party was ignored. The thousands who were turning up at rallies in the wind and the rain were ignored, as were the real people having real conversations about the state of British politics. As was Jeremy Corbyn, even when he was welcomed with respect and rapturous applause wherever he went – the Labour Party was pronounced dead on arrival by the mainstream media. For 616 days, it was reported that the Labour Party was over owing to Corbyn's disastrous leadership. Done. Finished. For ever.

This opinion culminated in the disastrous party coup attempt of June 2016. It has been widely reported that, just hours after the European referendum result was announced, Hilary Benn – the son of Corbyn's political mentor, Tony – was contacting shadow cabinet members and asking whether they would back a call for Corbyn to resign. Like many senior figures in the party then, he felt that Corbyn's lacklustre support for the Remain campaign had allowed the

Brexiteers to win. On top of previous disputes, they saw it as the final straw. After a phone conversation between the Labour leader and the then Shadow Foreign Secretary, Benn was sacked for disloyalty.

What followed appeared to be a well-planned coup attempt against a leader who remained incredibly popular within the party that would soon re-elect him, but was much less so among his own MPs. Many of Corbyn's critics maintain that the coup was 'spontaneous', but my own experience of that weekend suggests that it was anything but unplanned. Dozens of Labour MPs wrote their resignation letters, posting them on their respective Twitter and Facebook profiles one after another. On Sunday 26 June, Corbyn lost twelve members of his shadow cabinet on what was almost an hourly basis. First to go was Shadow Health Secretary Heidi Alexander, then Shadow Minister for Young People and Voter Registration Gloria De Piero, then Shadow Scottish Secretary Ian Murray. They were followed by the Shadow Education Secretary, the Shadow Chief Secretary to the Treasury and a host of other top jobs. None of these resignations was entirely surprising. In what seemed like a co-ordinated effort, the Sunday saw the resignation of a number of those who were seen as part of Labour's 'soft-left', such as Lisa Nandy (Shadow Energy Secretary), Owen Smith (Shadow Work and Pensions Secretary) and John Healey (Shadow Minister for Housing and Planning).

Nandy, Healey, Nia Griffith and Kate Green made a point of marking their resignations as from the 'centre left of the party' in a joint statement that they released after meeting with Jeremy Corbyn: 'Together with our colleagues from the centre-left of the party – John Healey, Nia Griffith, and Kate Green – we just met with Jeremy Corbyn to discuss the future of our party. We had hoped to leave that meeting with the confidence to continue to support the leadership in bringing the Labour Party together from within the shadow cabinet. During the course of the meeting, it became clear that this would not be possible.'

As the Parliamentary Labour Party moved to dispose of Corbyn, his supporters organised to defend him. At 6pm on the Monday evening, thousands gathered in Parliament Square for a rally in support of the Labour leader, having been given just a few hours' notice to attend. A cursory glance at the images of the rally show that Parliament's green was littered with young people, including one person carrying a sign in reference to Hilary Benn that read 'chat shit, get sacked'. John McDonnell tweeted from the platform that Jeremy Corbyn was 'going nowhere'.

Devoid of any ideas, the coup leaders moved to select their contender. I felt confident that Jeremy would increase his mandate whoever challenged him, but I wanted to do what I could to help ensure it would be as big an increase as possible. After their initial failure to unite behind one candidate, the Parliamentary Labour Party opted for Owen Smith as their knight in shining armour. Few outside the party knew much about him, and Smith's campaign was so bad that I often joked that it seemed like he was standing to lead a university rugby club rather than the labour movement. In a poll released shortly ahead of Corbyn's second leadership victory, 61 per cent of 18–24-year-olds were found to be supporting him. In fact, Corbyn won every single region and every single age group in the poll. It also showed that he would win across every section of the party electorate, from full members to registered supporters and union affiliates.

But I didn't vote for Jeremy Corbyn in the second leadership election. Yes – you read that right. It wasn't because of some sudden change of heart, but because I was denied a vote. Despite being a signed-up and subs-paying member of the Labour Party since I was fifteen (I actually joined against Labour rules when I was fourteen, but was later kicked out), I did not receive a ballot paper. This was something that I chased up as soon as it became clear I had not received my e-ballot. I had confirmation from Labour's HQ that my subscription was up to date and that there was no query with my membership.

I wrote about the issue for the *Independent* on 21 September, noting that:

> I was surprised when I didn't receive my ballot in the normal timeframe for this leadership contest. I contacted the party on 2 September to ask why. They said there had been an administrative error and that they would re-issue my vote for me. After ten days of hearing nothing, I got in touch again, only to be told that my ballot had not been properly re-issued but that it would be with me that week. At the start of this week, I still had nothing, and after a phone call today, I've been told that it's too late for me to vote now and there's 'nothing they can do'.

After posting my experience online, it became clear that scores of young people had found themselves in a similar position. Several friends contacted me to say that the same thing had happened to them, yet their Labour Membersnet accounts (a hub for Labour members to control their membership and check local activity) showed them up-to-date and as registered members. The search that I conducted on Twitter at the time also proved that a substantial number of young Corbyn supporters were concerned about being denied their vote. It was clear that radical reform was needed within the party. Fortunately enough, it was something that Jeremy Corbyn had already addressed:

> Our party needs to become a social movement again – with campaigning at its heart. To many younger members, meetings consisting of minutes, reports and internal business can be a bit turgid – they are to me too. We must inspire people – to get involved and stay involved and we must organise ourselves to ensure that is the case. Internally, Young Labour must have its own democratic structures – and be able to propose policy in areas affecting young people. Young Labour members don't just have the energy for full days on the doorstep, they have fresh ideas and a distinct perspective that need to be heard and debated. In a fast-moving world, we cannot go back to some mythical past in which we set policy only once a year at annual conference. I want our party to be at the cutting edge of engaging younger – and in fact all – members in setting the direction of our party. On demonstrations for free education, for peace and against austerity, I see thousands of young activists – and I want them to know that the Labour Party is their natural home.

Though Labour's popularity soared far higher throughout the 2017 general election campaign, it would be wrong to ignore the growth in support for Corbyn prior to the campaign itself. Indeed, Jeremy was appealing to young people before the general election had even been called. The Labour Party leader's approval with the under-25s during the first leadership election landed at a whopping 64 per cent. These were the first signs of the youth vote in the 2017 general election that surprised most pundits. Many more of these young campaigners and voters were brought on board by Corbyn in the years preceding the snap election, and were not disengaged from politics prior to the election as some thought. The political establishment may have reeled at what they believed to be Corbyn's inability to command the respect of the electorate, but in fact ordinary people were accepting his invitation to re-join the political debate.

As 23-year-old Labour Party member George Gillet told me: 'Not only did he interest people but he also sent a message that they were qualified to hold a political opinion – debates around values could involve everyone, they weren't exclusionary like the "market society" version of politics had been.' Again, while Corbyn remains central to this story, in the respect that without him none of this would have happened, he is better seen as a solution through which young people became their own champions. And, as 18-year-old Thomas Duffin, a Labour Party member from South Wales now studying in Nottingham, quite rightly notes:

> I support Jeremy because of how his politics has enlightened me and helped me realise that another world is

possible. Corbyn sets out achievable goals for a fairer and more equal society, and is not afraid to stand by those principles. His positions have remained unmoved for his entire career and he stays committed to the same principles of empowering real people, fighting imperialism, and demanding radical change to solve radical problems. He has an unvanquishable fire to solve the injustices of our current system, and approaches the world with a passion to make a change that other leaders had left behind. He is different to what we've seen in recent years, and that makes him such an important figure.

Some have suggested that his approach to young people during both Labour leadership contests was often exclusionary, focusing only on those who were already in the party. I would argue that while Corbyn's political language was aimed at those already involved in the machinery of the Labour Party, he learned much from engaging with our generation. And many of his detractors added the contradictory argument that Corbyn was involving too many from the outside of the party.

These were the kinds of arguments that led the Labour Party to the grotesque chaos of a Labour executive (NEC) taking its own members to court to ensure that they could not vote in the second leadership election in August 2016. One of those members, known only as 'FM', was a teenager. After a ruling at the court of appeal, the five victimised Labour Party members were ordered to pay at least £30,000 of the Labour NEC's legal costs. Fortunately, the Labour rank and file, incensed with a ruling that resulted in more than 130,000 members and supporters being excluded from the second leadership ballot, rushed to raise over £90,000 to assist with this burden. So paranoid had the belief in an entryist plot become that the Labour Party establishment saw fit to go after a teenager inspired to play a part in politics. This was rather unsurprising, however, given that some Labour Party grandees were keen to prevent Corbyn from even appearing on the ballot paper the second time around.

The young joiners who got involved with Labour's leadership elections knew exactly what they were getting into. Yet, senior members conformed to a political discourse that insists on telling young people that they are a disgrace for not engaging with politics, while simultaneously stressing their naivety when they do. These comments and opinions were deeply hurtful to the young people who didn't just vote, but campaigned and argued passionately for Corbyn's leadership. However, it was Jeremy Corbyn and his team, working from a position of meaningful commitment throughout his time as Labour leader, who were able to pivot a long-mocked policy of youth engagement towards the country at large.

Though the young are often criticised for being passive, only getting involved in campaigns for things that directly matter to them, Corbyn was able to bring them in and get them involved with wider issues. People felt as though they could proudly campaign under the Labour banner, rather than doing so under disparate groups and societies. Young people took to both social media and the streets to bring Corbyn's radical message to the wider public. If establishment commentators had taken the time to look, they would have seen that this story did not begin with the 2017 general election campaign, but rather way back when he was elected as Labour leader in 2015. It was at this point that it became clear to me that politics would not be the same as it always had been. Like many young people, I remember the feeling of dread when the 2015 exit poll was released. It felt as though Tory rule was being engrained into the British political system. Corbyn's election as Labour leader was so radically different to everything that we had seen over our own lifetimes that it was clear things were going to change.

SMEARS AND PROPAGANDA

The ordinary voices that would power a resurgence among the young spent the two years prior to the 2017 general election being mocked for suggesting that Jeremy Corbyn's appeal could change the face of British politics. At the same time, the establishment were given a spectacular position in the limelight to pontificate about the irrelevance of any socialist appeal while also downplaying the idea that young people might bother to vote.

It is easy to see why the dramatic increase in those registering to vote received little attention when you consider how the media commentators were reporting on the situation in the run-up to Labour's astonishing result. The very people who should have been enquiring about the staggering rise in young people wanting to get involved and have their voices heard were instead busy trying to push the idea that Corbyn was the least popular politician for a generation.

Though impossible to calculate the numbers at any single Corbyn event, the press photographs and television footage speak for themselves. Whether it be at a rally or a campaign day, what we see time and time again is the image of an old, grey-haired and bearded man being listened to by fresh-faced and beardless young people. The most poignant moments of Labour's election campaign were those when the young engaged with the Labour leader, from the creation of the 'Oh, Jeremy Corbyn' chant at Preston Park to the rather trivial – yet endearing – moment when Corbyn left the BBC leaders' debate and headed straight to a gate where he was greeted by the crowd. 'Are you okay, guys?' he said to a group of Cambridge students at the gate.

'Do you want a Pringle?' they replied.

'It's ours to win,' the Labour leader would later tell the rapturous crowd that had assembled to greet him.

Despite young people rushing to meet Corbyn wherever he went from the early days of the first Labour leadership election, many refused to believe that he was actually popular with them. Conservative MP Chloe Smith made this point in an article published in the *Daily Telegraph* in October 2015, in which she made some extraordinary claims about the link between young people and Corbyn. The headline – which she would not have written – read: 'Jeremy Corbyn's in for a shock when he realises how Conservative young people are.'

It certainly would have been a shock if it had been true. In the body of the article, Smith's writing made for enlightening reading. 'Shhhh, don't tell anyone,' she began, as if some Tory public relations guru had given her a briefing on how to open an article in the most condescending way possible, 'but most young people don't care about Jeremy Corbyn. The Labour leader and his throwbacks don't care about the overwhelming majority of the country, nor its future. They have a vision rooted in the past. Their ideas won't create a single job, nor build a single house. Socialism won't serve today's young.' Smith was blinkered in her analysis. She seemed to believe that young people not only detested Corbyn, but also that they felt alienated by the politics and the vision that he represented. It was a staggering misreading of what was happening.

As Conservative politicians struggled to come to terms with Corbyn's popularity, so too did right-wing commentators in mainstream publications. Jacob Furedi, writing in *GQ* magazine just a matter of weeks prior to the 2017 general election under the headline 'Why do young people hate Jeremy Corbyn?', serves as such an example. 'Young people need real politics' was the charge of Furedi's article – suggesting that Corbyn's offer was nothing other than shallow posturing. But this also exposed the confusion on the right when it came to their attacks on the Labour leader. In one breath, you had a Conservative politician criticising the party for advocating a solid version of socialism, and yet in the other you have a Conservative commentator accusing the party of preaching a vacuous form of nothingness.

This type of criticism only helped to boost his popularity, rather than hinder it. So baseless were many of the attacks on the Labour leader that they appeared to come from every angle, on every topic, usually with no attempt to attack his argument or positions, but simply to discredit his name. He was smeared for being a dogmatic and extreme socialist, but was also guilty of offering too little. He was criticised for ignoring Labour's northern heartlands while also failing the metropolitan bases on Brexit. He was condemned for backing pensioners' rights and simultaneously attacked for offering hope to young people. The greatest weakness of Corbyn's critics has always been their failure to agree on what he was doing wrong. In the end, the right simply indulged in a relentless campaign of personal denigration that made Corbyn's young supporters more emboldened than ever.

Fortunately for the Labour Party, Chloe Smith was entirely wrong. In fact, she could not have been more wrong if she tried. Young people disagreed with her analysis and the 'youthquake' that Jeremy Corbyn sparked led to a ten-point surge in the Labour Party's vote share. This figure even betters Tony Blair's performance in Labour's crushing 1997 landslide.

For all that, it wasn't quite enough. Labour Roadmap, a group of Labour activists, note that despite this rise the electoral system punished Corbyn's surge. Though the party won 40 per cent of the vote in the 2017 general election, they won only four more parliamentary seats than they did in 2010, when Gordon Brown managed to secure just 29 per cent of the vote. Opponents of the Labour leader have suggested that the explanation for this contradiction rests with the stockpiling of votes in seats Labour already held. But such an analysis does not explain why Labour managed to win seats in university towns long safe in Tory and Liberal Democrat hands. Nor does it help to explain why Labour was successful in securing seats such as Kensington – where Corbynista candidate Emma Dent Coad won the richest borough in the world for a party promising to take more in tax from the wealthy.

The fact that Labour won only four more parliamentary seats in the 2017 general election masks the huge loss of seats in Scotland since 2010, when the party won forty-one parliamentary constituencies north of the English border. Labour managed to claw back some support there, but it was in England and Wales that the Labour Party was able to make its 2017 gains. Young people contributed to the surge in seats where they were most important and least important. Even when Labour was seen as safe, young people still turned out in greater numbers to vote. The resurgence of the youth vote was therefore not solely down to a belief that voting could change things, but rather that it mattered.

Though young people represent only a slice of the increase in Labour votes, it is hard to see how such a hike could have been achieved without the energy and enthusiasm of the young, working hand-in-hand with older and more experienced volunteers. Laura McAllister, Professor of Public Policy at Cardiff University's Wales Governance Centre, told the BBC the day after the election that 'it looks like we have seen a kind of parity now between young people, 18–25-year-olds, voting in almost the same numbers as the groups that have historically always been relied upon to go out and vote which is the fifty-five to sixty-five.' And so, despite all the media comment, even though he didn't win the election, Jeremy Corbyn did manage to reverse a worrying trend in British politics. Whereas previously young people were not just failing to turn out at the ballot box but were also becoming disillusioned with democratic institutions altogether, now – thanks to him – they had become a vital part of the process once more. This change looks certain to have a big impact on politics in the future.

But most commentators were not interested in understanding where Corbyn's support was stemming from and how the Labour leader had achieved this dramatic change. Labour's alternative vision came under sustained criticism from the opposition and the media alike, and one could argue that no Western politician in recent history has been subject to the same level of hostility. Even though Donald Trump received much scorn from the press – throughout the Republican primary race and even the presidential election – the fact that Trump was seen as a joke ensured that he received more balanced press coverage. The same treatment was not afforded to Corbyn. My generation understood these attacks within the context of Jeremy Corbyn: The Underdog. We had only ever seen him vilified by a political class and a media that we do not trust. This was an important factor in convincing young people that Labour's message must have something good to say given those who lined up against it.

There was a simple reason for this. My generation's first major engagement with the British press was the phone-hacking scandal, where we learned of journalists hacking the phones of politicians, celebrities and, in one particularly tragic case, the phone of murdered schoolgirl Milly Dowler. In that context, it is no surprise that young people place little trust in journalists today. Indeed, most young people do not buy newspapers at all, getting their news from other sources. Those who do read them, however, did not accept the smears and attacks produced on the front pages of Britain's right-wing newspapers throughout the election campaign, because we knew such papers to have been guilty of vile acts before. As far as we were concerned, we were being sold lies by well-known liars.

The idea that the press has treated Corbyn unfairly is hardly a radical one. It isn't even some internet meme that has been concocted by his supporters, as many in the media would wish us to believe. A report published by the London School of Economics entitled 'Journalistic Representations of Jeremy Corbyn in the British Press' looked at the way the Labour leader had been written about by mainstream outlets. The foreword to the report notes: 'As media and communication scholars we have been troubled by the problematic way in which the British media has systematically attacked Jeremy Corbyn ever since he came to national prominence in the summer of 2015.' Writing for the *Independent*, the head of the report, Bart Cammaerts, noted the following:

> As our analysis of the journalistic representation of Jeremy Corbyn's first two months as party leader in eight national newspapers demonstrates, this did not apply to Corbyn. Our rigorous and statistically representative analysis concluded that when it comes to the coverage of Corbyn in his role as leader of the opposition, the majority of the press did not act as a critical watchdog of the powers that be, but rather more often as an antagonistic attackdog.

The report found that 75 per cent of press coverage misrepresented Corbyn and the political positions that the Labour leader supported, that more than 50 per cent of all news reporting about Corbyn was 'negative or blatantly antagonistic' and that 67 per cent of all opinion pieces and newspaper editorials were deemed to be the same. The report concluded that such bias was not limited to the traditional right-wing press and that those supposedly on the left wing also considered him 'too left, unrealistic, unelectable'. For example, there were almost as many negative articles in the *Guardian* as there were positive. There were more negative articles in the *Independent* than there were positive – in fact, there were more negative articles than there were balanced ones.

Further research by the Department of Film, Media and Cultural Studies at Birkbeck University and the Media Reform Coalition, based at Goldsmiths, found 'clear and consistent bias in favour of critics of Jeremy Corbyn' when it came to those asked to appear on political television shows. Though there are strict rules surrounding impartiality, the report found mainstream news bulletins featured voices critical of the Labour leader twice as much as they did voices that supported him. This feeling was not just reserved for academic reports. YouGov polling conducted in 2016 found that 51 per cent of British adults believed that the media coverage of the Labour leader has been 'deliberately biased'. A study conducted after the 2017 general election from the Centre for Research in Communication and Culture at Loughborough University also found that newspapers and broadcasters were biased against the Labour leader throughout the campaign.

The extent of press bias in the UK remains staggering and worrying, though unsurprising given the ideological persuasions of the British press barons. Despite Labour's success at the 2017 general election, it would appear that this will not change anytime soon, but whether this matters or not (given the rise of social media) is a different question altogether. Corbyn's supporters are probably best concentrating on engaging with new media than they are trying to reform a morally bankrupt industry that is trusted by just 25 per cent of the British public, according to a survey by Ipsos MORI. Ultimately, in my view, the attacks served only to strengthen the idea that Jeremy Corbyn was offering a real alternative to our broken political system. Whether out of arrogance or editorial pressure, these journalists pushed on, giving the Labour Party the best gift they could possibly offer: an abundance of energetic and active young people desperate to deliver them a bloody nose.

A New Media

Corbyn's message found a home in the new media and his unashamed support for the downtrodden young was given a boost by the ordinary voices that Theresa May claimed she had been so desperate to hear when she surprised everyone by calling a snap general election in 2017, having previously insisted she would carry on for the full term until 2020. She soon discovered that she wasn't necessarily going to like what they had to say to her.

'I'm angry,' shouted Kathy Mohan, as the prime minister shuffled her way through Abingdon marketplace in Oxfordshire. She didn't know it at the time, but Kathy's words would help to turn the tide of the entire general election campaign. After weeks of meeting Conservative Party activists behind closed doors, often in quiet locations, the prime minister's foray into the open confirmed the view of many: Theresa May simply wasn't the confident political maestro she had been marked up to be. Having already been subjected to heavy criticism for her apparent lack of interest in engaging with the general public, the reason for May's reluctance to do so was made obvious during this walkabout in Oxfordshire.

Mohan, who, it was reported, has struggled with mental-health issues and a borderline personality disorder, was able to confront the prime minister over the Conservative Party's decision to slash the Personal Independence Payment (PIP) afforded to disabled benefit claimants. Though May had thus far avoided a major public gaffe, Kathy ensured that she would be quizzed in front of the busy marketplace and in the glare of the national media – and she did not come across well. More importantly, this moment was shared widely on social media to an audience of millions. 'Do you know what I want? I want my disability living allowance to come back . . . I can't live on a hundred pounds a month,' she argued.

Encapsulated within this disruption was a narrative that would soon become central to the election campaign: faced with the average man and woman on the street, Theresa May simply did not know how to act. Forced to shift her campaign strategy from invitation-only events to public appearances after coming under heavy fire from the Labour Party campaign, May had been propelled into uncharted and uncomfortable territory. Mohan told the *Guardian* that when she saw the prime minister, it was obvious 'she didn't want to talk to anyone who wasn't up her street'. This moment in a small market town – which had for the past seven years been a Conservative constituency – became yet another failure in the Tory campaign. May's refusal to hold a televised debate with Jeremy Corbyn, her hostility towards a largely sympathetic press and her failure to interact with the public earned her the unaffectionate nickname of the 'Maybot'. As anybody in politics will tell you, it is rare for the adoption of any nickname to spell anything other than disaster. As it turned out, Kathy Mohan's disruption would not be the worst part of Theresa May's day.

That afternoon the prime minister had been scheduled to take part in a live Q&A event on Facebook Live with ITV political editor Robert Peston. The week before, I told those in Corbyn's office that May's refusal to debate needed to be attacked head-on. I had strongly urged them to use May's LBC phone-in event – held the week prior to this Facebook Live session – as a chance for Jeremy to put a question directly to the prime minister through a 'hijacking' of her scripted programme. Unfortunately, it was not possible to get Corbyn on the phone with the prime minister for the LBC event. But there was another way. The openness of Facebook and its new 'Live' format allowed for anyone to pose a question to the prime minister – including the leader of the opposition.

A comment was posted on the broadcast from Jeremy Corbyn's official Facebook account off the back of my original LBC suggestion: 'Hi Theresa May, as Prime Minister you have served your elite friends by giving them tax cuts while wages have stagnated, house-building is at its lowest since the 1920s, there are 20,000 fewer police on our streets since 2010 and the NHS is in crisis. Do you not think the British people deserve to see us debate, live and on TV?'

The post soon went viral. The video of the moment that Theresa May was asked the question by Robert Peston was uploaded to Corbyn's official Facebook account and became one of the most watched videos of the general election campaign. In total, 4.8 million people saw the video. The 'gatecrashing' then went on to receive mainstream media attention. The *Independent* splashed 'Jeremy Corbyn ambushed Theresa May during Facebook Live event', the *Daily Mail* noted 'Corbyn hijacks Theresa May's first EVER Facebook Live' and even the BBC commented on Corbyn's 'surprise' questioning of the prime minister through unconventional means. Ben Sellers, who helped orchestrate Corbyn's first leadership campaign in the summer of 2015, cited the Facebook Live event as a pivotal moment of the digital campaign which 'placed Theresa May in a very difficult situation ... and cemented the embarrassment for her'.

Though this was a spectacle, it was an important one. At each point in the campaign, the Labour leadership refused to give ground to May on the issue of the debates, which we will see was a hugely important issue for younger voters. In doing so, Corbyn chipped away at her 'strong and stable' rhetoric while at the same time discrediting those who labelled him as a weak and ineffectual leader. The audacity of this 'hijacking' was further proof of his desire to work outside the traditional rules of modern politics. And the media was more than aware of this – that is why they called it a 'hijacking' and an 'ambush', not an 'intervention' as they usually would. Corbyn's activism was interpreted as some form of guerrilla tactic, but it was not. The Labour leader merely used the tools of communication by which the young and the less powerful were getting involved. He had done it in a way that was perfectly in tune with their own methods of response.

Digital media and Labour's social media campaign played a huge part in assisting this strategy. On the same day that Corbyn submitted his question during May's interview, Labour-supporting page 'Red Labour' reached 1.8 million people by promoting the video. Its reach was organic, in the sense that it did not pay for any advertising, and it didn't pay to boost its posts to a wider audience pool. Similarly, the Corbyn-supporting grassroots site 'Jeremy Corbyn for PM' reached nearly 900,000 through organic posting.

Within a context where the Conservative Party spent £5 million on Facebook advertisements alone, such organic reach was crucial for the Labour campaign. Though Labour was spending roughly £1.2 million on similarly targeted adverts, it was the grassroots element of Labour's digital campaign that made all the difference. Just as the Labour Party has always relied on the generosity of its activists to knock on doors and get out the vote, new digital activists have been relied upon to provide the online fightback at a time when the Conservative Party was outstripping Labour Party spending on digital advertising by a margin of at least four to one. Grassroots Twitter accounts such as @ScouseGirlMedia, @Rachel_Swindon and @EL4JC received praise throughout the election campaign for reaching as many people as the establishment press and its commentators. Hundreds of new online activists sprang into action to assist with disseminating Labour's hopeful message.

Ben Sellers, who returned to work for the Labour leader on digital media for the general election campaign, had seen how this sort of grassroots support could be utilised to help defeat the Conservative Party in key seats. Talking on the importance of social media, he wrote in 2015:

The #JezWeCan social media operation has been the driver for much of the positive aspects of the campaign: getting across Jeremy's central messages of respect and encouraging debate rather than a beauty contest, stimulating the engagement of volunteers and attendance at the huge events all over the country. Most importantly, we have been able to blunt some of the media attacks by relentlessly pushing a positive message and creating alternative sources of news for our supporters.

It was a similar strategy that Sellers sought to bring to Corbyn's social media output for the 2017 campaign, along with the core digital team. In the days following the general election result, Sellers spoke to me about the impact of the social media campaign waged by the Leader of the Opposition's Office (or LOTO, for those in the know). The figures for Jeremy Corbyn's online reach are staggering. The weekly reach of his Facebook page averaged 24 million. That's 24 million UK Facebook users (over a third of the entire country) who were accessing Labour Party campaign material through his official page. His Twitter profile tells a similar story. Throughout the campaign, his tweets generated nearly 343 million impressions, averaging at 6.6 million per day. What is also staggering is the number of people who didn't just see Corbyn's posts online, but actively engaged with them, either by sharing, liking or commenting on the post itself. On Facebook, engagement averaged at 9.48 million shares, likes or comments per week. On Twitter, Corbyn's posts were re-tweeted a total of 1.5 million times throughout the campaign, averaging at 29,700 per day. The scale of this online campaign and the importance of it cannot be overstated.

Buried below such stunning statistics is the fact that it was my own generation that was most engaged by Corbyn's online campaign. On Facebook, 24 per cent of his total 'likes' at the end of the election campaign were from people under the age of 24, with 55 per cent of followers of the page being under 34. On Twitter, 36 per cent of his followers at the end of the general election campaign were under the age of 24 and a massive 67 per cent of followers were under the age of 34.

Sellers stressed that these figures are associated with Corbyn's personal accounts – not the official Labour Party pages. He also argued that Corbyn's social media output 'was in stark contrast with the Labour Party's social media output'. Sellers told me that the official Labour Party digital campaign was 'safe' and 'boring'. He went as far as to explain that official Labour Party staffers were 'overtly hostile to the fact that Corbyn, or our ever-increasing membership base, could be a tool to get our message out'. He told me that senior Labour Party staffers in Southside made the job much harder.

It is clear from my interview with Sellers that the atmosphere in Labour HQ was far from conducive to a positive campaign focused on the leader's appeal. Sellers cautioned that there is a need to remain aware of the fact that the 'Labour Party machine' had been quick to 'establish their narrative' after the election result was declared, citing the example of a *Guardian* article that gives credit to 'Labour Party' staffers of the official accounts – even though all evidence contained within the article had come from Corbyn's personal accounts.

My conversation with him made clear that there are still many fights to be waged and won within the party. It is obvious that Sellers wishes to challenge the idea that it was the Labour Party machinery that developed a dynamic campaign: 'Just like many other parts of the internal party struggle, we now have an opportunity to change the internal dynamics.' Sellers saw the job of the team to 'fill in the gaps' of the Labour Party output, while inspiring people with video content in a 'similar way to that which Bernie Sanders had'. The figures referenced above speak for the success of this strategy. Writing for the *Guardian*, Robert Booth and Alex Hern noted that having discussed the online campaign with 'digital strategists close to both camps', it was clear that 'Labour outflanked the Conservatives in the battle for votes on social media for the first time in a major election'.

The strength of groups outside the leader's office and Labour's Southside HQ was also of paramount importance (Southside is the building within which the Labour Party is based; it became known as 'Darkside' to many through-out the general election campaign, owing to its hesitancy to engage with what they believed to be the myth of Corbyn's popularity). Momentum's online content was seen by a third of the UK's Facebook users. The group reached nearly 13 million people in the final week of campaigning, promoting anti-cuts and pro-Labour messages as well as boosting Corbyn's profile further, with the leader featuring heavily in their videos and images. New campaigning tools such as My Nearest Marginal also helped to push activists into areas where campaigning was most needed. Sam Jeffers, co-founder of Facebook advert monitoring group 'Who Targets Me?', said that many Facebook news feeds became a 'sea of red' mainly owing to organic sharing, with friends tagging others and promoting content on their own profiles. It has been reported that Momentum spent as little as £2,000 on paid advertising, meaning that it achieved such an amazing reach without the need for massive expenditure.

Key figures from Bernie Sanders' primary campaign were also drafted in to advise the group, such as Erika Uyterhoeven, a 30-year-old campaign organiser from Boston, and Jeremy Parkin, a 27-year-old Sanders campaign organiser. One of the main changes brought about by this advice was the move away from emailing Momentum members to texting them with a personal message. According to the *International Business Times*, Momentum contacted 400,000 people on election day through WhatsApp with reminders to vote. Once labelled as a lynch mob, the young and enthusiastic organisation defeated a Conservative Party machine steeped in cash and experience.

While the print media continued to be dominated by pro-Conservative headlines, the most-shared stories online painted a different picture. The *Press Gazette* noted that 'only five out of the top 100 most-shared stories on social media were pro-Tory'. Searching the Buzzsumo database for the top 100 most-shared stories, the *Gazette* found that

'45 were anti-Tory/pro-Labour, 46 were neutral ... and five were pro-Tory'. Though many of these most-shared stories came from the traditional liberal media, such as the *Guardian*, the *Independent* and the *Mirror*, there was also a surge in the activity of what has been dubbed the British 'alt-left' media.

The rise of sites such as the Canary, Evolve Politics, Novara Media, the Skwawkbox and others is testament to a group of activists willing to challenge the existing right-wing bias in the British media. These sites, and the people behind them, have been roundly denigrated in traditional media circles. There is an irony in a biased right-wing press criticising the hyper-partisan sites for their backing of Jeremy Corbyn, given that many of the same journalists will go out of their way to offer great support to the Conservative Party and to Theresa May. Often portrayed as 'activist-journalists' by a mainstream press ignoring its own obvious Conservative activism, such sites have given a voice to those on the left who might otherwise have been denied one – and their success is often down to the engagement of young people online.

Once seen as an 'echo-chamber' where people spoke only to those with similar views, the 2017 general election proved the growing power of social media as never before. As Buzzfeed's political editor Jim Waterson tweeted on the morning of the election result: 'Doubt these results could've happened without big shift in media readership.' Though the Westminster media bubble seems unable to grasp what the spread of this new media means, everyday people on Facebook and Twitter clearly do. There is an obvious appetite for a source of information that is unashamedly left-wing and supportive of this new movement.

Despite still selling millions of copies a day, the traditional print press must now come to terms with the fact that it has lost its monopoly on deciding election results. The 2017 general election campaign demonstrated that normal people can take control of the political media agenda. Whether it be articles written by Thomas G. Clark (the author behind the 'Another Angry Voice' blog), which were often read by as many people who purchase the *Daily Mail* and the *Sun* on any given day, or the fact that millions watched Momentum's campaign videos, it is clear that the political media landscape has been changed for ever.

As these groups come to realise their power and influence, it is likely that they will only get stronger. This will be a worry to a Conservative Party that remains reliant on the traditional arm of the media, which is haemorrhaging influence and power as people – particularly the young – move towards new forms of media.

But, as with any modern campaign, Corbyn's success was not based on clicks alone. On the same day that May was ambushed by an angry voter and by Corbyn online, Labour's campaign cemented its direction as 'for the many, not the few'. Speaking at Brudenell Social Club in Leeds – the same event mentioned earlier where thousands of students turned out to hear the speech, some climbing trees to get a glimpse – Corbyn outlined his plan for a 'fat cat' tax which would charge a levy on big businesses, banks and Premier League clubs offering massive pay packages to employees. On the back of his plan to introduce a 50 per cent tax rate while protecting 95 per cent of the population from any tax rise, the announcement was timed perfectly. On the very same day, he pledged to scrap the 1 per cent pay cap for public sector workers, vowing to 'help underpaid and overworked nurses suffering at the hands of Tory austerity'.

Though criticised by some for 'stealing' Tony Blair's campaign slogan, Corbyn set out to do something that Blair had never truly attempted: placing the populist rhetoric of the campaign at the heart of party policy. 'For the many, not the few' became so much more than a slogan. It was both the embodiment of his political career to date and the foundation upon which every single day of Labour's campaign was built. The formula seemed simple: Corbyn would rally against a distant elite in one breath and promise a fairer settlement for the majority of voters in the next. As May's 'strong and stable' rhetoric receded to annoying background noise, Corbyn's decision to repeat Labour's phrase resonated with young people who had felt ripped off by the few for too long.

Though Corbyn engaged in a similar tactic to May's message discipline, the key difference was that it was natural and sincere – it was also much more positive, while May's 'strong and stable' message was easily ridiculed every time her party displayed any divisions or uncertainties. Corbyn had been rallying against the powerful and speaking for the powerless for decades. No matter what the policy, or whether he had been labelled a terrorist sympathiser the day before by the Tories, Corbyn's support for the downtrodden was written in history, so there was no doubt he was for helping 'the many'. Reaffirming this point at every stage of the campaign using that simple messaging was hugely effective, but simultaneously completely overlooked by the commentariat that still – even after the result – largely refuses to accept Corbyn's personal appeal, especially to the young.

Before the election, young people had been seen as unreliable voters. A Tory candidate 'with over ten years' Commons experience' had told the *Huffington Post* that the 'under-30s love Corbyn but they don't care enough to get off their lazy arses to vote for him!' The quote became a perfect tool for engaging young people and reminding them of the view that the Conservative Party held of them. Morgan Paulett, a 17-year-old from Caerphilly who was too young to vote in the election, told me that he did 'the next best thing ... I campaigned, I knocked on doors and I shared memes unendingly'. Rather innovatively, Morgan also told me that he 'strapped a "Vote Welsh Labour" sign to my dog and used him as party propaganda'. I am happy to report that the dog is now known affectionately as 'the Labourdour'. Sarah Huxley, a 22-year-old who told me she had 'never been more inspired by a politician', noted that she went canvassing having not done it before: 'I have never done anything like that before but I genuinely believed Corbyn was worth it.'

Christopher Holinshead, a 23-year-old Labour supporter, told me that he didn't just vote for Corbyn, but that he 'wrote articles on an independent blog I created ... shared endless amounts of articles and was one of many who went out on election day to make sure people voted'.

Even though Alex Dixon – a 25-year-old campaigner who joined the Labour Party because of the election – told me that campaigning in his home seat, the Tory stronghold of North Hertfordshire, would be 'a bit like screaming into the abyss', he still took time to campaign online, reaching places where his activism was more useful. This was quite common. Paul Collins, another young voter, told me that though he campaigned 'on the streets of Runcorn trying to ensure Labour voters actually voted', he decided to travel to the 'Weaver Vale constituency with people I had never met before, joining a hundred-strong team of volunteers' to 'help Mike Amesbury take his seat off the Tories'. Paul called this 'one of my proudest moments'.

With Corbyn having inspired so much enthusiasm and activism among the young, it is no surprise that those who decided to do something to support their beliefs should find themselves in the firing line as well.

THE CORBYN 'CULT'

We now know that it was politics, not Trotskyite coercion, that brought millions from my own generation to the Labour Party's cause. As James Smith, a 27-year-old support worker and music teacher from Leeds, told the *Guardian*: 'For the first time, I feel powerful.' The young people who hailed Jeremy Corbyn's principles also welcomed the power that he had promised to place in their own hands. James notes later in the same interview: 'I hope everyone understands it is not actually about him as a "saviour", but that it's about everyone coming together and looking after each other.'

Yet this idea that young people see Corbyn as perfect – a line of attack against the Labour leader that has grown somewhat boring – continues to be used, even in the aftermath of the 2017 general election. Nick Cohen, a writer so incensed about Jeremy's ever-rising popularity that he simply appears to write the same sort of denigrating article every week, even decried the 'leadership worship' after Labour's 2017 party conference. Most other commentators opted to note the exceptional way in which innovative ways of reaching out were discussed.

To suggest that all of Jeremy Corbyn's supporters think he is perfect is a fallacy. Sure, he's hugely popular – try to get the man from a stage to a car and watch the crowds swarm to take a selfie with him. But young people are not blind to the darker moments of the previous two years. As Morgan Paulett told me: 'Don't get me wrong, I don't think the man is perfect.' There was a real sense of frustration when it was announced that Corbyn would 'relaunch' himself in January 2017 with a speech on the issue of freedom of movement, which seemed more reminiscent of Ed Miliband's 'controls on immigration' than the migrant-rights supporting history of the Labour leader. Though quickly explained and altered, the day was dubbed the 'day of chaos' and left many feeling confused and worried about Labour's immigration plans. There was a real feeling of disappointment ahead of the clarification. Young people voiced this online and, in applying pressure, Labour's line was changed in a matter of hours. I voiced my concerns privately, as did many others. There was no point in giving further oxygen to the mainstream press, which had jumped on this embarrassing day as another way of forecasting Labour's doom. It was again easier to label the man a freak leading a cult than to understand exactly why this unlikely politician maintained the respect of his supporters even when he wasn't getting everything right.

Examples of this attitude abounded. Hadley Freeman led the charge on the cult rhetoric during Labour's 2016 leadership campaign, when Owen Smith challenged Corbyn for the top position. Those of us who sided with Corbyn were smeared daily. The *Guardian* published Freeman's article that compared Corbynistas to the Manson murders. In response to the article, the leadership hopeful – who was live-tweeting his anniversary dinner at the time – told his following that 'We're dancing to the Cult at the moment. Who says irony is dead.' This charge has been used repeatedly to discredit the movement that championed Corbyn's politics.

The critics seemed to ignore the fact that a political cult is usually created as a tool by the leaders themselves. As Dr Robin Bunce notes: 'Cults of personality tend to be imposed from above rather than emerging from below … the cult of Lenin and the cult of Stalin were deliberately manufactured and fed to the Soviet people through a Communist-dominated media.' I think it is vital to dismiss the idea that Corbyn was working to broadcast a self-created cult of personality. His popularity was built from the bottom up. The spontaneous chants of his name, the cheering at Glastonbury, the young people climbing through windows to hear him speak at campaign rallies – all of it was produced by the people, not by the leader or his team. It is hardly as though he has a hype artist accompanying him to whip crowds into a frenzy. He doesn't need one.

And so, while Zoe Strimpel at the *Telegraph* was shaking in her boots at Corbyn's 'terrifying' development of a cult of personality, and the *Independent* was writing editorials that boasted 'Jeremy Corbyn's cult of personality puts Labour ever further from power', ordinary people were building their own appreciation for a man more interested in helping them than in helping himself.

When young people were labelled as being part of Corbyn's 'cult', what we were actually being called was stupid and susceptible. Our voices were being depicted as naïve and detached from the reality of political discourse. Our support for him was seen as nothing more than blind loyalty to an old man pushing a strange doctrine. Our campaigning and determination was lumped with some of the worst instances of political history. So keen were Corbyn's critics to trample his movement that abuse became the norm. And this was not from the Tory Party – it was also from people supposedly on our side.

When Labour MPs – both on the backbenches and the frontbench – moved to attack him in the aftermath of the European referendum, it felt like the final blow for young people. I told the *Independent* at the time: 'The feeling among most young people who voted for Corbyn is: enough is enough. Corbyn has moved to replace the dissenters and has begun forming his new shadow cabinet. The membership remains rallied behind his leadership and continues to support his mandate. If the "bitterites" in the party want a leadership election then so be it: Corbyn will be elected again.'

He was duly elected again and once more the smears seemed only to help his cause. The utility of the mainstream sneering is something Jeremy Corbyn has come to appreciate himself, as he highlighted during his 2017 conference speech when he attacked the 'overwhelmingly hostile' coverage of Labour's campaign and his own leadership. He noted that 'the day before the election, one paper devoted fourteen pages to attacking the Labour Party. And our vote went up nearly ten per cent.' In a sign of his strength, he went on to do what few political leaders have done before, goading the press with a question to the editor of the *Daily Mail*: 'Next time, please could you make it twenty-eight pages?'

On a philosophical note, it is easy to understand why older commentators rushed to deny the importance of the rise of the young. The fresh-faced and energetic young people that came to Corbyn's aid stood in direct opposition to everything those commentators held to be true. Long-held political 'truths' suddenly collapsed before their own eyes. But they were not just political truths that they believed in, they were ones that they themselves had created.

These hacks – most of whom are middle-aged white men – spent their careers feeling that they did not have to speak to the young, or understand them, as they didn't seem important or relevant. They now see that world view directly challenged and falling away before them. The young remind them of their own mortality, of the very physical limits placed on their own power and influence. It is therefore completely unsurprising that they spend so much of their time and energy battling to preserve that which they have created, as well as challenging the notion that the young have come to change everything. To admit that the time of extreme uneven capital accumulation, mass support for privatisation and an acceptance of tax dodging is coming to an end is to admit that they are also soon to be rendered obsolete.

This can be a hard thing to accept – impossible even. To welcome Corbyn's popularity as something other than idol worship would be to accept that the age of triumph for the narcissistic political individual is over in the UK. Doing so would reduce the importance of these hacks who do not do their jobs out of a love for serving the public, but for serving themselves. It is their name on the byline after all. But politics has changed. Their books will not be part of the canon. Everything is going to change and that is something they will do their best to oppose. The liberal commentariat is experiencing the current political crisis in a metaphysical and personal way. To accept the rise of the young is to accept the end of the old.

Chapter 2

SurpRise

May's Conceited Moment

Most young people who were engaged in politics before the 2017 general election will remember where they were the moment that 'May to make Downing Street statement' flashed across television screens – and, perhaps for the first time for a snap election, millions of smartphone screens too. As soon as I read the alert, I was sure that we were heading for a general election. I tweeted that an election announcement was on the way and that we needed to be ready. After a few minutes of trying to take in what was to come, I called a few friends who I knew would be interested in the shock news. I gathered my thoughts and considered the magnitude of what was about to happen. Most people I spoke to on the phone that morning were terrified by the prospect of an election. 'It's all over,' said one of my pessimistic comrades.

Jeremy Corbyn happened to be appearing on ITV's *Good Morning Britain* when the election was announced. The questions that were asked of him were pretty much par for the course, concentrating on Labour's position in the polls and his 'failing' leadership. Corbyn told the programme that the polls would turn, noting that 'I think people will begin to see that actually what we are saying makes a lot of credible sense'. Presenter Piers Morgan tweeted: 'I can't help liking @jeremycorbyn. Like Wenger, a decent principled man – but seems oblivious to reality.' Just like Corbyn, Diane Abbott faced similar criticism later in the campaign.

It isn't the first time that Morgan has spoken too soon. We now know that the reality Corbyn touched upon would come true, after all. Having insisted for the previous months that an election would not happen, the temptation of the Conservative position in the polls had become too much for Theresa May. Political journalists were sent into a frenzy; Andrew Sparrow speculated on the five reasons May was about to call an election on the *Guardian*'s Politics Live blog. 'The polls, obviously' was the first point he noted, citing a YouGov poll released the previous day which showed the Conservative Party on 44 per cent and Labour on a terrifying 23 per cent. Sparrow also drew attention to the 'Best Prime Minister' figures released in the same poll: 50 per cent of people opted for Theresa May, 36 per cent opted for Don't Know and just 14 per cent picked Jeremy Corbyn. It was a striking point that brought home the task that Labour faced.

Moments after May's announcement, Corbyn welcomed the challenge of an election, noting that the Labour Party looked 'forward to showing how Labour will stand up for the people of Britain', but others were less positive. Former Home Secretary Alan Johnson announced that he would not be standing for

re-election and Tom Blenkinsop, a longstanding critic of
Corbyn (known to some on Twitter as Tom Blenkinsblock for
his propensity for blocking opponents online), refused to stand
in the election, noting his 'irreconcilable differences' with the
Labour leader. John Woodcock, a critic of the Labour leader,
announced that he would stand as a candidate under the Labour
Party banner, but would not endorse his leader, telling the
media that he would 'not countenance ever voting to make
Jeremy Corbyn Britain's prime minister'.

Outside of his own party, Corbyn once again found himself on the receiving end of widespread criticism from all
wings of the political establishment. Matthew d'Ancona – a
weekly columnist at the *Guardian* and chairman of the Bright
Blue think tank – wrote that he never thought he 'would feel
sorry for Jeremy Corbyn, but today I do'. Simon Jenkins also
noted that 'an election under Jeremy Corbyn is certain to be
painful' and that Labour's 'sad flirtation with the archaic left
should soon be over'. Jonathan Freedland wrote that May's
'gamble' was really 'about the surest bet any politician could
ever place'. By contrast, the often-mocked Shadow Home
Secretary Diane Abbott told BBC News: 'This won't be the
first time the polls have called a general election wrong.' As
excitement gripped Westminster, Conservative MPs looked
forward to their assumed increased majorities and Corbyn's
internal opponents scrambled to raise their 'serious concerns'
about his leadership.

There was, however, the small matter of agreeing to the
general election. Since the introduction of fixed terms, a
two-thirds majority in the House of Commons had to agree
to an early election. Ignoring the naysayers, Corbyn took

to the airwaves to tell the British public that he would vote for May's snap election, proclaiming to the nation that he wanted 'to lead a government that transforms this country and brings real hope to everybody'. Eight Labour MPs went on to vote against it, although admittedly for a number of different reasons.

But while the politicians and activists were ready for and excited by a third crucial visit to the polling stations in two years (and a fourth inside three years in Scotland), many outside that world felt very differently. The best rejection of the election came from outside Parliament. In a now viral clip, Brenda from Bristol responded to BBC reporter Jon Kay's question of how she felt about the election with a shout of 'Not another one!'

However, in a poll conducted by IMC for the *Guardian*, it was found that 55 per cent of respondents supported the call for an early election, with just 15 per cent opposed. Taking a closer look at this original data, young people aged eighteen to twenty-four were more likely than any other age group, except for those aged sixty-five to seventy-four, to support the idea of an early general election, with 60 per cent in support and 25 per cent against. So unthinkable was the idea of Labour coming anywhere close to power that when the pollsters asked respondents which outcome they predicted to be most likely, there was not even an option to back a Labour majority. Though an underdog since the day that he was elected leader of the Labour Party, Corbyn entered the general election with the same odds of victory as he did in September 2015.

But, despite the views of the pessimists, the pundits and

the pollsters, a movement rallied behind its leader. Pop star Lily Allen tweeted after the announcement was made: 'YOUNGERS, the Conservatives don't care about you. Your future is in YOUR hands, but you HAVE to register to vote.' Little did she know what such a call to arms would start. Like Allen, my first thought when May called for a snap election wasn't that the polls were accurate or that Labour was headed for a historic and final defeat, but rather that with the right campaign, Labour could do something brilliant. My immediate concern was that the Labour Party would respond to this announcement in all the wrong ways, and I feared that their campaign would most likely take a cautious approach – concentrating on saving seats rather than winning them. And, indeed, the Labour Party establishment decided to do just that. The truth is that much of the fight in the election did not come from the Labour Party machine, which (owing to its internal polling data) decided to fight a largely defensive election campaign, directing resources to seats which had upwards of a 10,000-vote majority. Fortunately, the party leadership and the membership decided to adopt a different approach.

A day after this first poll was released, Tony Blair made his first intervention in the campaign with a comment that would have seen any other Labour member removed from the party. He appeared to be encouraging Labour supporters to back the Liberal Democrats in seats where an anti-Brexit candidate had a chance of being returned, telling the BBC: 'What I'm advocating may mean that [voting Liberal Democrat].' He had previously given an interview in which he stated that he 'didn't understand' why Corbyn was so popular with Labour members. This comment was made at a time when Blair was said to be considering a return to British politics. The fact that the former prime minister believed that he was the answer to our current problems showed that he was certainly right about failing to understand modern politics at all.

Blair's political vision – which seems frozen and fixed in 1997 – was never going to be appealing to the 2017 electorate, and certainly not to today's young voters. Nevertheless, the stir that was caused by Blair's comments stood as a timely reminder of the sway that Labour's grandees continued to hold over the way the party was addressed in the media. Blair would make more interventions as the campaign steamed ahead, along with other members of the New Labour aristocracy. Fortunately for those crying out for a transformational campaign, the Labour leader ignored these calls and took to the streets of Britain with an optimistic message that would, in turn, inspire young people like no political campaign ever before.

Despite that, the first week of Labour's campaign ended in disarray. Party grandees had moved to denounce Corbyn, the party slipped further in the polls and the narrative of the campaign looked cemented around the idea that Labour was finished. But as those in London's Labour HQ seemed to be losing their heads, campaign sessions across the country were reporting strong turnouts. Young people took to social media to share the fact that they were becoming engaged with their local Labour Party, taking to the doorstep as well as social media to ask others to back the party they believed would work best for them. Even without the hope that would be built over the next few weeks, an enthusiasm was bubbling under the surface, with Labour's supporters already feeling fired up by the opportunity of offering the British people a genuine alternative.

While the reporting of the Labour Party's positioning and strategy was sensationalised, Theresa May's quiet refusal to participate in live television debates marked the first major mistake of the Conservative campaign. Since the election, the prime minister has, somewhat ironically, claimed that her 2017 campaign lacked real 'debate' – despite the fact that she refused to take part in any such debate. As Jeremy Corbyn aptly replied to this point on Twitter: 'I was at the debates. Where were you?'

Televised debates are far more important to young people than many appreciate. In 2010, the Reuters Institute for the Study of Journalism argued that among 18–24-year-olds, 'a special relationship [was formed] with the TV debates compared with more jaded older people'. This research also found that 55 per cent of 18–24-year-olds who were asked stated that the televised discussions helped them come to a decision regarding their vote. Professor of Political Communications at Leeds University Stephen Coleman, who was also part of the 'Leaders in the Living Room' study, told a number of political editors that the debates proved that 'an appetite exists ... nobody should be left out'. This was certainly the case with young people. Ipsos MORI polling after that year's general election found that turnout among those under twenty-five had increased by some 7 per cent. Though hardly seismic in comparison to what happened in the recent 2017 election, an increase is always welcome and it is clear that the television debates helped get young people to the ballot box, or at least involved and engaged with the political process.

The prime minister's argument against participating in the debates was that she was more interested in speaking to people on the streets of Britain, suggesting that she could reach more people on foot than she could via the airwaves. Gripped by a belief that May was the people's prime minister, set to romp to victory with a landslide greater than Tony Blair's, the move received widespread praise outside of the left. But May's decision was a blessing in disguise for Jeremy Corbyn. The refusal to participate in the debates allowed the Labour Party to build a narrative around the Conservative Party's unwillingness to engage with the young.

They portrayed May's arrogance as astounding and her decision made her seem even more distant to young people. It suggested that May was more interested in knocking on the doors and talking to the grown-ups she would encounter in the day than reaching the youngsters sitting in the living rooms as their parents answered the door to party canvassers. It wasn't so much that the Conservative Party was bad at reaching out to young people, but rather that they simply did not seem interested enough to even try. It was the perfect example of how young people have felt patronised, and thus turned off, by the political system. The idea that politics should be left to the adults has been a prevailing view in British politics, despite young people being just as much affected by the issues that politicians seek to address. With the belief of certain re-election, she decided that this kind of job interview was not necessary. While she was happy to run a presidential-style campaign of May vs Corbyn, she wasn't willing to engage in a presidential debate with him.

Initially, Corbyn announced that he would stay away from

the debates unless the prime minister attended. I disagreed with this, but I understood the concern that proponents of this position held. Former leader Ed Miliband's performance in 2015 was seen almost as a joke – with David Cameron's absence making the whole thing look like an audition to be the prime minister's understudy. But Corbyn was always going to be different. That is why I was so pleased that those opposed to his participation changed their minds in time for the second debate, with the Labour leader 'showing up' on the day and challenging May to do the same. Though often overlooked, I believe this distinction played an important part in cementing the support that he achieved among the young.

POLITICAL FAILS

Young people remember the 2010 general election for a variety of reasons, with many that I spoke to suggesting that it was the television debates that sparked their political interest. This was, of course, the time of 'Cleggmania'. The then leader of the Liberal Democrats, Nick Clegg, seemed like a smart and affable character, offering the young a chance to escape the burden of ever-growing university debt, following the introduction of tuition fees by the Labour government, which had risen to just over £3,000 a year by then. But Clegg betrayed his younger supporters as soon as he came to power as deputy prime minister in coalition with the Conservatives; rather than cutting them entirely, as stated in his party's manifesto, he accepted the Tories' decision to almost treble them to £9,000. And, as the researchers behind 'Youth Participation in Democratic Life: Stories of Hope and Disillusion' – an analysis of the rise in turnout at the 2015 general election – suggested: 'Young people are not bored with politics; they are fed up with feeling that those who "do" politics do not care about them.'

Nick Clegg brought some young people back into politics, but his deal with the Conservative Party would send engagement plummeting once again. In an exclusive poll for the *Daily Mirror* at the end of 2010, young voters who had backed the Lib Dems during the election turned to name him the 'most deceitful politician in the country'. The *Mirror* noted that the poll came 'just eight months after the election's first TV debate when Mr Clegg became the most popular political figure since Sir Winston Churchill'. Never has there been a greater fall from grace. In reality, Clegg should have been a casualty of the 2015 general election. The anger that students felt towards the Liberal Democrat leader should have been enough to topple him from his position as an MP, but instead it seems that Miliband's 'austerity-lite' approach, and his pledge to reduce tuition fees from £9,000 to £6,000, simply was not radical enough to bring those still disillusioned with the political arena out to vote. The offer of piecemeal change was not enough to enthuse the young after this great betrayal.

Despite his apology, Clegg went from being a figure who had inspired an increase in youth engagement to one responsible for them feeling more turned off from politics than ever before. It was almost like an extreme betrayal. Young voters were used to being let down by politicians who were not interested in talking about them, but not so much with politicians who had actively approached them and promised to speak on their behalf. To engage with young people in such an obvious way, signing pledges to scrap tuition fees before trebling them, was a serious smack in the face to those of us who had been urging people to get out and vote. It was the final confirmation to many that voting changed nothing, that all politicians were the same.

His party saw its seats slashed from fifty-seven to just eight in the 2015 election, though Clegg did not receive his final punishment until June 2017, when he lost his Sheffield Hallam seat as young people – galvanised by Corbyn's message of hope – used their vote to end the career of a man who they believed had lied to them.

Another way to assess young people's newfound engagement is to compare their involvement in the snap election to Labour's 2015 campaign under Ed Miliband's leadership. The overwhelming view of young people seems to be that Miliband's desperation to appear centrist or 'pragmatic' was unconvincing and damaging. As James Raftery – a 16-year-old activist and 'proud citizen of Leigh' – told me:

Young people didn't feel fired up by Miliband because he is an establishment politician. He represented the things that most young people weren't: posh, rich ... Now, Jeremy is nearly seventy, but in the way he engages with young people and the way he speaks to people you can tell he is young at heart and understands the plight of young people. Miliband did not truly understand the hardships that young people had to go through and he didn't understand that young people have increasingly no prospects for the future. Miliband was someone that young people just couldn't rally around because he didn't have young people's best interests at heart.

Joe Bailey echoed this sentiment, telling me: 'I didn't feel fired up by Ed Miliband because I don't agree with his politics. I am not a fan of centrists and I believe they have pursued goals that have led Britain to the state it finds itself in today.'

Jeremy Corbyn was often accused by commentators in the mainstream press of simply preaching a platform of 'turbo-Milibandism', whereby Labour's policies were not that different from the Ed Miliband era. It appears that young people would reject this idea entirely. Sam Harper argues that it was Corbyn's radicalism that engaged him after Miliband failed to do so: 'He wasn't interesting and different enough. I like the man but I wasn't compelled to vote for him as he didn't inspire real change like Corbyn does. Corbyn has always been the opposite of the Conservatives in every aspect and never wavered in his belief, and that means a lot to our generation.'

An earlier respondent supported this view when I asked about it: 'I would say it's a combination of many different factors. At the heart of it all, I think he didn't offer enough of an alternative to what we already had. He was criticised for not seeming strong enough and I think that was partly it.' Whereas Corbyn created an overarching narrative that offered its support to the many, Ben Blackwell – a 24-year-old who joined the Labour Party during the 2015 leadership election – told me that Miliband's failure was down to the fact that he did not do this:

Ed Miliband may well have had left-wing values and probably would have been a good prime minister, but he didn't create a coherent narrative. It's very difficult to

throw your weight behind someone who can simultaneously speak out against zero-hours contract but then also
do nothing to challenge the narrative of austerity. With
such a schizophrenic message, all that was left was to fight
the election on personality and he seemed far too robotic
to win anyone over in this way.

Where Corbyn made the issues of young people central to
Labour's campaign, the young people I spoke to believed
that Miliband wasn't all that concerned with them. Anjelica
Cleaver – a 22-year-old who campaigned with Momentum
during the election – told me: 'Ed Miliband wasn't talking
to young people … there also wasn't the massive support
from celebrities and figures young people respect and listen
to. Grime artists were able to translate Jeremy's policies in a
whole new way and show how they were relevant to a lot of
young people who wouldn't have cared before.'
In this sense, Corbyn met young people where they were
and on their terms, rather than forcing them to adapt to a
political system that didn't represent them. Many commentators questioned whether, in 2017, they would do the same
as they did during the 2015 general election and fail to show
up to the ballot box in significant numbers. I appeared on
Sky News Sunrise, just ten days after Theresa May called
the election, to discuss new research which suggested that
an increase in young votes had the potential to swing the
entire general election. YouGov showed that, despite being
more than twenty points behind in the overall polling, the
Labour Party was storming ahead with those under the age
of forty. Indeed, YouGov revealed that Labour would win

the election by some margin if only young people voted. I told the news reporter interviewing me that 'if we can inspire young people to vote, the result of this election could be very, very different'. This view was widely seen as nothing more than a joke at the time.

People took to Twitter to mock what I had said, as if the 'lazy' young could ever bring themselves to get out of bed and vote. But, in the four weeks that followed my interview, my belief that young people could change everything was consolidated by a major increase in those registering to vote, and that resulted in more casting their vote than ever before. The government's own data shows that over a million people aged between eighteen and twenty-four registered to vote between 18 April and 22 May. A rather astonishing 246,000 young people registered to vote on the final day alone – a testament both to Corbyn's inspiring message and the laborious practical work done by political groups such as Momentum and RizeUp, as well as non-partisan bodies such as Bite the Ballot. The number of people registering to vote on 23 May was record-breaking. At 8.30am, over 5,000 people were using the government's website to register. So much for not being bothered enough to get out of bed. This trend continued throughout the day. The prevailing view that young people didn't vote out of a lack of interest in politics began to unravel.

For the sake of comparison, consider this: on the corresponding cut-off day for the 2015 general election, 137,000 young people below the age of twenty-four had registered to vote, and similarly 132,000 did so on the final day of registration for the EU referendum. What the 2017 general election represented was a marked upsurge in young people determined to have their say. Looking at the government's own data, we can be certain that the 2017 general election registration period saw many more 18–24-year-olds claiming their right to the ballot paper than we had seen in recent election campaigns.

It can be assumed that such an incredible drive was achieved to the dismay of the Conservative Party. In the week prior to the registration deadline, the Conservative Party and Theresa May did not use their social media platforms even once to encourage people to register to vote. Much of this may be down to an understanding by the Conservative Party that the youth vote was shifting in Corbyn's favour. By contrast, David Cameron encouraged the young to get involved, but he did so with the backdrop that the previous increase in young votes was split fairly evenly between Labour and the Conservatives.

That was never going to be the case in this election. A study by the Press Association found that the Labour Party was urging people to claim their ballot in more than a third (36 per cent) of all online posts. In the same period, Jeremy Corbyn's personal accounts were calling for the same in more than a quarter (26 per cent) of all posts. Theresa May's personal social media accounts were never used to encourage people to register to vote. The last time that the Conservative Party supported voter registration attempts on Twitter was during the 2010 general election – now three general elections ago. In response to this, Corbyn's personal Facebook page posted an image of a Facebook search on Theresa May's account for the phrase 'register to vote', which returned nothing, or, more accurately, the response: 'Sorry, we couldn't find any results for this search.' This post was shared over 17,000 times and 'liked' by some 37,000 people.

As the prime minister seemed to be crossing her fingers for a reduction in the overall turnout figures, Jeremy Corbyn – rather than relying on any instance of fate or luck – was instead endeavouring to engage as many new voters as possible and to marshal their support. In turn, the Labour leader would be greatly rewarded for taking the risk to engage those who had previously felt disenchanted with the political system. As the statistics demonstrate, it was Corbyn who had his call to arms answered.

Despite opposition, the leadership made a very clear decision to target the young vote. An adviser within Corbyn's office told me that young people were 'vital' for Labour's election result. 'By inspiring young people, we expanded the electorate, got more people interested in politics, registered to vote – and keen to actually go out and vote. In several seats across the country, it appeared to have made the difference,' they said. The decision to focus on this area was met with some hostility. 'There was definitely opposition from those who thought it was a waste of time and resources. When we were advocating a voter registration drive, we were told by some party officials: "Non-voters don't vote; that's why they're called non-voters."' The criticism of the idea of chasing non-voters was well established. In many ways it was the snobbery of rejection.

The typical argument in British politics has always been that the number of those who vote and those who don't is fixed; that is to say that if 15 million people didn't vote last time, 15 million will not vote the next time. From this assumption, the Labour Party had always believed that it must appeal to swaying Conservative voters if it wished to win power. In turn, what this really meant was that the Labour Party had to look and act more like the Conservative Party so as to win those undecided votes in the middle. But this did not work for Ed Miliband in 2015, when he attempted to balance what was evidently his desire for a left-leaning manifesto with the 'pragmatic' understanding of the fact that he needed to win over millions of Conservative voters if he was to become prime minister.

Jeremy Corbyn took a very different position and adopted a very different strategy. He and his team unashamedly decided to speak to non-voters, roughly a third of the population who had disengaged with the political process. Many of these voters were young people – some who had only just become old enough to vote. As we now know, the decision paid dividends. This was another stark contrast to the 2015 campaign, with the Labour Party changing its entire electoral strategy within the two years since Corbyn became Labour leader.

Labour had been thought vulnerable in seats where UKIP had done well in 2015, especially in the north, because it was assumed many of those voters would turn to the Conservatives, who had brought them the EU referendum and a Leave outcome, and thus give them a landslide. In fact, many of them had voted Labour before 2015, and Corbyn believed he could win them back by appealing to the disaffected.

What we saw at this last election was that many UKIP voters supported Labour out of sheer frustration. There is a reason why the 2015 election saw a seemingly strange number of former Liberal Democrat voters switch to UKIP. In my opinion it had little to do with policies and more to do with politics. After the coalition, the Liberal Democrats had positioned themselves as a party of government rather than a party of protest, and with such a decision the protest vote needed to find a home elsewhere, which was why some turned to UKIP in 2015. Labour made a calculated and wise decision in chasing this protest vote, and it did so successfully given that the UKIP vote split roughly 50/50 between Corbyn and May, despite the Tories' pro-Brexit-at-any-cost stance.

One does not need to ask what would have happened if Corbyn had adopted a strategy similar to Ed Miliband's in 2015. To have had a Labour leader whose career is so well documented as radical and outspoken attempt to pander to the Conservative vote would have been disastrous. Fortunately, Corbyn and his team ignored the warning calls of those who believed the decision to focus on the young would bring ruin to the party at the election. Those voices now find themselves somewhat marginalised from a new political mainstream they still fail to understand.

Started from the Bottom

The prevailing view of Labour's certain doom was supported by its tragic position in the polls. At the end of 2015, just some months after Jeremy Corbyn's first landslide Labour leadership victory, he had a net approval rating of -41 per cent with polling agency YouGov. At the same time, Opinium found that though 28 per cent of people had a favourable view of Corbyn, 56 per cent didn't – giving the Labour leader a net approval rating of -28 per cent.

One poll by ComRes for the *Independent on Sunday* put the Conservatives fourteen points ahead of Labour as early as February 2016 – a time when David Cameron was still leading the party.

Throughout the following four months, the Tories would lead Labour by a maximum of nine points, with some polls showing the Labour Party ahead by three. The overall picture, however, was still that the Conservatives were well ahead, despite the crises within the party, and the looming EU referendum, which we had been told would rip them apart. In fact, Cameron's lead in the polls was nothing compared to the victory march Theresa May appeared to be on once she became leader in July 2016.

Once the Brexit vote was confirmed, double-digit leads for May's party became the norm of British politics. In several polls, Labour was trailing by up to twenty-five points. Much of the discussion concerning these failings was raised by a Fabian Society report released at the beginning of 2017, which determined that Labour had no chance of winning the next election. Highlighting the issues of Brexit, further losses in Scotland, and the supposed unpopularity of Jeremy Corbyn, the report argued that the Labour Party was doomed to fail. This view was the basis upon which the election coverage took shape and it infected the beliefs of many in the party who were critics of Corbyn. Most commentators were united in the belief that he would lead the Labour Party to a tragic end.

The first poll of the election campaign, released on 22 April, showed the Conservative Party heading for a historic landslide. An Opinium poll for the *Observer* suggested that the Conservative Party had doubled its lead over Labour in the week since Theresa May announced the election to nineteen points. Had this poll been right, with the Conservatives on 45 per cent and Labour on 26 per cent, the snap election would have returned May to power with a majority above and beyond 100 seats.

Labour was nowhere to be seen and talk of removing the leader – even at this late stage – received some traction. BBC *Newsnight*'s economics editor Emily Maitlis tweeted the question: 'Is there enough time to remove Jeremy Corbyn?' as praise was heaped on Yvette Cooper as a potential saviour ahead of polling day. It is important to remember that this was a serious position just eight weeks before he would rewrite the rules by refusing to do politics the way he was supposed to – with a key element of this refusal being his determination to appeal to the young. And it wasn't Twitter trolls who mused about his ability but establishment commentators who became entrapped with viewing every story and every development in the election campaign through the lens of Corbyn's leadership.

Conservative victory at the election was not even a point to be debated; the only thing that needed to be considered was what the size of the victory would be. May looked set to change the political landscape, with a large majority set to give her free rein over Brexit negotiations and the opportunity to turn the clock back by reintroducing grammar schools and lifting the ban on fox hunting.

Most took the opinion polls as their guide to the mood of the nation. Commentators often muse that British opinion polls are reliable because they are more often accurate than not. American polling expert Nate Silver challenged this belief prior to the UK general election under a byline that correctly predicted that 'if they [the polling agencies] underrate Labour ... Theresa May's majority is at risk'. Silver summed up his position in the article by stating:

> Given the poor historical accuracy of UK polls, in fact, the true margin of error on the Labour–Conservative margin is plus or minus 10 points. That would imply that anything from a 17-point Conservative win to a 3-point Labour win is possible. And even an average polling error would make the difference between May expanding her majority and losing it.

The volatility of opinion polling in the UK, coupled with generally inaccurate historical predictions close to election day, led Silver to believe that everything was to play for. Those of us who argued this at a time when Labour found itself miles behind in the polls were not taken seriously as some responded fatalistically. However, the energy of Labour's later campaign and the enthusiasm with which Jeremy Corbyn sold the message proved that campaigns do matter. Or, at least, they do now. Over the course of the campaign, people steadily moved towards Labour's message, with young people flocking to the Labour leader's aid.

Whether on the campaign trail, at rallies or online, Corbyn's role in engaging young people remained central. A key adviser within the Labour leader's office told me that 'Jeremy has an authenticity and honesty that appeals in an age of deep, and often justified, cynicism about politicians'. The fact that his record demonstrated a serious support for young people also mattered. The adviser told me that 'on key issues for young people, like tuition fees, he's always supported them [young people], whether it meant opposing Tory governments or Labour ones'.

However, some have subsequently claimed that there was a different reason why young people turned out to vote in 2017. This narrative claims that young people took part in the election to oppose and overturn Brexit, but this is simply disingenuous. Though true that those under the age of twenty-five were more likely to have voted to Remain in the European referendum, not every young person did. The idea that Corbyn has come to betray young people over the European issue is nonsense, but it is a line that has been used time and time again, even by figures such as Vince Cable, who wrote in the *Guardian* that while true that Labour won over young voters, 'it is betraying them on Brexit'. Rather than betraying anybody on Brexit, Corbyn opted to back the Remain campaign, despite his Eurosceptic views, from the moment he was elected Labour leader. Other politicians did not make their minds up until the day that a certain column was required for a newspaper.

In rejecting 'the adage that young people are fools who will eventually come to their senses and vote Tory', Corbyn provided a platform that won the hearts and minds of young people, Alex Fletcher told me. Taking the time to speak to young voters proves once and for all that the cause of all this engagement was not dissatisfaction with the European referendum result or a hatred of the older generation, but rather the way in which Jeremy Corbyn consciously chose to engage with young people.

THE VIRAL MANIFESTO

Though May's refusal to debate was important in changing the trajectory of the election, it was not the attacks on the Tories that bolstered Corbyn's Labour. Instead, it was the hope and the optimism scrawled across every page of Labour's manifesto 'For the Many'. An article that I wrote for the *Independent* during the election campaign was picked up as one of the most shared mainstream press pieces throughout the period. In the article, I noted how previous opponents of the Labour leader could no longer pretend that the manifesto did not deliver:

> This manifesto is the manifesto of Labour's future. The ambitious plan to scrap tuition fees, to offer a cradle-to-grave national education service and to invest in our communities tackles the real problems at the core of our social and economic turbulence. In setting out to tackle our low-productivity and low-skills economy, Corbyn's radical vision will deliver a country that can stand proud of its ability on the world stage once again. That, during Brexit, is more important than ever ... this pitch to the British people is one to be proud of. Beyond the rhetoric, it is a genuinely transformative plan that lives up to its slogan. For people who believe in society rather than individualism, these specific, economically sensible, compassionate policies make sense. Whatever you think of Jeremy Corbyn, that can't be denied.

After weeks of trailing enticing policies, such as the pledge to rule out any tax increase for the bottom 95 per cent at the expense of the top 5 per cent, or the decision to scrap hospital car parking charges, the Labour manifesto was leaked in its entirety. The person behind the leak remains unknown. I have been given so many different names of who was responsible that it has become something of a joke to even try to pin the blame on one individual. Those from opposing sides of the political spectrum within Labour's internal politics point the finger at each other. The prevailing view, however, appears to be that the leak was manufactured by Corbyn's opponents, owing to one major policy that some believed would sink the Labour leader once and for all: the pledge to scrap university tuition fees.

In many ways, whoever leaked Labour's 2017 manifesto isn't important. If it was done by a political ally, then it was a masterstroke of political strategy. If it was leaked by a political opponent with the aim of hurting the Labour leader, then it backfired. It is risible that the professional political class within and outside of the Labour Party felt that Corbyn's bold and ambitious offer to the young would be one that destroyed his future. The policy that invigorated hope and a genuine belief in the Labour brand – partly tainted by New Labour's introduction of the fees in the first place – was initially seen by some of Labour's insiders as a short-sighted and misguided announcement that would only push people away from the party.

Labour's manifesto was popular for two reasons. The first was undeniably its content. The second was the way in which social media moved to change the narrative from 'Labour in chaos' to 'look at Labour's truly transformational offer to the country'. Thanks to new connections between the top of the party and grassroots social media organisers and activists, lines were not just given to those hitting the airwaves but also to online activists with a reach of millions. And so, Labour's manifesto became the talk of the town, so to speak.

Much of the reason for this rests with the fact that for the first time in many years there seemed to be a real and stark difference between what people were being offered by the two major parties. Fed up of 'all politicians being the same', few could say that the 2017 general election presented voters with this problem. Fired up by the fact that Labour's manifesto promised something different, not just to the Conservative manifesto but also to our current seemingly irreversible trajectory, young people embraced both the contents and the dissemination of Labour's viral message.

And there was one other important factor in the campaign. Research from the London School of Economics has shown that a personal visit from Jeremy Corbyn during the general election campaign helped to further increase the swing from the Conservatives to Labour. In the seats that he visited and held campaign events, the swing stood at an average of 19 percentage points. Comparatively, those seats not visited by the Labour leader saw a swing of 9.8 per cent. In short, Corbyn's visits helped to double Labour's swing. Those who dismissed the incredible crowds at Corbyn's rallies across the country have had their own false narrative fundamentally challenged. Corbyn addressed the issue of his rallies in his final campaign speech in Islington, telling his home crowd: 'This is the new mainstream. The new centre ground. The place where people actually are. The things they want, not what the establishment and their media mouthpieces say they should want.'

Despite the polls that consistently pointed to Corbyn's unpopularity, the staggering turnout at his campaign rallies stood as one sign that this might not be the case. At the end of the 2017 general election, veteran broadcaster Michael Crick claimed that the turnout for the Labour leader's rallies was something that hadn't been seen since the time of Winston Churchill. But, in what was typical of the opinion towards Corbyn's rallies, Crick followed up by saying that he expected the Tories to win comfortably despite the large crowds.

Just a few days prior to Crick's tweet, Corbyn had addressed an enormous crowd in Gateshead. The press images taken on the day show just how many young people were attending such events. The same can be said of the crowds at Corbyn's rallies in Birmingham, York and Derby. Every event was flooded with thousands of people, with the Labour leader often forced to make several speeches to appease all of those who turned out to get a glimpse of him, whether in the actual venue booked, from the roof of that venue or even in the car park. Corbyn ensured that Labour's message was delivered personally. Contrasted with the scripted and staid community centre events that Theresa May would attend, in a room packed with previously selected Tory supporters, these rallies felt electric.

It was something that had been happening prior to the election, though. Throughout both leadership elections, Corbyn attracted massive crowds. The mainstream comment on the events noted that he was preaching to the choir, with many arguing that he was slipping into a 'bunker mentality'. Those who attended the rallies were often criticised for taking part in idol worship – but what is clear is that the clips and images of Corbyn being greeted by thousands everywhere he went helped to convince people that he was a serious contender. As the energy of the campaign grew, so too did the crowds. As May's strong and stable rhetoric disappeared into irrelevance, the Labour message of 'For the Many' was reflected in the crowds that Corbyn would address. In many ways, the slogan was given life by the fact that it appeared to be reflected in the campaign that his team orchestrated.

During the campaign, some said the Labour leader had visited too few Labour seats, instead opting to go to Tory seats such as Battersea (Labour's 89th target seat), Warrington & Leamington (Labour's 70th target seat) and Colne Valley (Labour's 43rd target seat). Despite being criticised for visiting these seemingly unwinnable Tory seats at a time when the press was adamant Labour would lose seats even where they held a 10,000 majority, they went on to win these seats, with some thanks clearly owed to Jeremy Corbyn's visit, if the research from the LSE is to be believed.

Peter Johnson, a 19-year-old student, supported that view when he told me that Corbyn was 'incredibly important' when it came to engaging young people; indeed, he goes as far as to say that it was 'all down to him'. But this isn't some sort of belief in a messiah either, as Peter explained: 'I think it's the policies above all else, but those policies wouldn't be there without him ... no other leader could have energised young people like he has.'

Andrew Jenkins, who is twenty-one, told me that 'his views and ideals are what people our age have been crying out for and we've finally been given them'. James Barber, who was unable to vote in the last election as he was seventeen, said: 'Corbyn appeals directly to us by talking to us like we are equal to adults and like we have the power and can make a difference.' Charlotte Cochrane, another 17-year-old unable to vote, supported this idea too, arguing that Corbyn was 'very important' and that his focus on the young was 'instantly engaging'.

Given such testimony, we need to ask the question of just how effective was Corbyn at bringing out the young to vote, and how much did the young really get behind him?

Chapter 3

THE REVOLUTION

THE YOUNG TURN UP

As we've seen, not many believed that young people would buy into Jeremy Corbyn's message and vote in greater numbers than ever before – establishment hacks least of all. But of those who did, the idea was welcome to only a restricted few. So it came as a great irony that members of the liberal media – seemingly so proud to valiantly defend the ideals of freedom and democracy – engaged in a campaign to deter young voters altogether. While accusations of voter suppression would be hyperbolic, it is clear that right-wing journalists galore fantasised about keeping young voters at home.

There is no better example of this than the supercilious and idiotic feature that was published in the *Sun* newspaper on the day of the general election. Titled 'Shhh . . . let your kids lie in', the piece openly encouraged parents to do the 'civic thing' and 'stop them [young voters] from voting'. Now, the left is often accused of having a serious lack of a sense of humour, and I am not suggesting that this piece in the *Sun* was a serious piece of political journalism, but the condescending tone in which it was written is enough to note it as an attempt to deter voters.

'If it's a boy, buy him a deluxe edition of the Grand Auto Warcraft Call of Duty XIV video game,' stated the guide, before going on to encourage introducing kids to 'skunk' or 'LSD' in order to 'keep them occupied for the day'. The guide was weird. If it was supposed to be funny, it failed, and if it was meant as entirely serious, it failed on that basis too. I hope that all it achieved was to embolden those young people who read it to go out and vote. Many of them certainly did.

The turnout of young people in the 2017 general election stands as a testament to the determination of Jeremy Corbyn's team to engage those who had been locked out of the political process. Reports regarding turnout still vary widely. The truth is that we will never know exactly how many young people voted – the secret nature of the ballot ensures this. However, we do know how many young people were registered to vote. Working from the fact that 1.5 million new young people registered to vote we can gather some idea of the scale of engagement.

The earliest estimations pointed to a 72 per cent turnout of voters aged between eighteen and twenty-four. Later, Sky News placed the figure of young voters in this age group at 66.4 per cent, nearly matching the overall figure of 68.8 per cent turnout reported on the night. This approximately matched earlier polling that suggested 66 per cent of young people were determined to vote. According to Ipsos MORI, the turnout for voters of the same age grouping in the 2015 election was just 43 per cent. The British Election Study, produced for each general election, is a reliable guide for gauging estimated turnout by age at each election. For reference, the last time that turnout of 18–24-year-olds was as high as in 2017 was the 1992 election, where it was estimated to be 67.3 per cent.

Looking back a little further, it is estimated that 63.9 per cent of 18–24-year-olds turned out in the 1983 election and more young people voted for Thatcher than Michael Foot. This is another example of where the supposed similarity between Corbyn and Foot is rubbished. Ipsos MORI estimates show that 42 per cent of 18–24-year-olds backed Thatcher's Conservative Party in 1983. Thatcher managed to win more of this vote than Michael Foot, at which point just 33 per cent of 18–24-year-olds backed Labour. There is clearly a massive difference in the way that young people perceived Foot and the way today's young people perceive Corbyn.

Another interesting comparison is what happened during Blair's 'cool Britannia' election of 1997, a time when young people were supposed to have been brought to politics under the wave of change. In 1997, the British Election Study reported that 54.1 per cent of 18–24-year-olds voted, and this figure fell in every single election that Blair stood as prime minister. In 2001, just 40.4 per cent of the same age range voted, and in 2005 (after the invasion of Iraq) that figure had fallen even further to only 38.2 per cent. These figures help to shine a light on just how staggering the 2017 turnout was.

Surveys conducted by Ipsos MORI after the general election came to a similar conclusion and placed the overall turnout of voters aged 18–24 at 64 per cent – the highest turnout for this age group in twenty-five years. The 2017 general election saw the turnout figures for the youngest group rise to the same level as those aged 25–34 and 35–44. Bobby Duffy, the managing director of Ipsos MORI's Social Research Institute, stated quite clearly that he believed the rise in turnout among young voters was a 'big factor' when it comes to explaining Corbyn's success.

It is worth repeating that we will never know exactly how many young people voted – but the polling and research all serves to support the anecdotal evidence of a huge increase in young people turning out. The Electoral Commission report on the 2017 general election states that turnout of the under-34s was 'likely to have been around 11 percentage points higher than in 2015'. The report notes that there was a 'greater turnout and an increased level of awareness among younger people of both the election itself and of the parties and candidates standing at the poll'.

It should also be noted that 8 June 2017 marked the 104th anniversary of the day that Emily Davison, a tireless campaigner for female suffrage, hurled herself in front of the King's horse, which was racing in the Epsom Derby, to demand votes for women. The reason this anniversary needs to be recorded is because of the particular role that women played in ensuring Corbyn's success. Ipsos MORI found that 'there was a difference between young men and young women' where 'among 18 to 24-year-olds, Labour increased its vote share much more among women than men'. Their polling revealed that a staggering 73 per cent of women aged 18–24 voted for the Labour Party, compared to just 18 per cent for the Conservative

Party – a rise of 30 per cent for Labour on the 2015 general election result. Though Labour still won comfortably among men of the same age group by a margin of 52 per cent to 36 per cent, there is quite a marked difference here between the genders that should not be ignored.

As a man, I am conscious of the fact that my own experience cannot account for this part of Corbyn and Labour's rise at the 2017 general election. Fortunately, many of the passionate and active young women who rallied behind him took the time to note the reasons that they themselves decided to do so. Drawing on their accounts, it seems that some saw Corbyn's challenge to the establishment and the status quo as a challenge to the patriarchy. It wasn't just in the election that Corbyn's appeal was greater among women than men. High levels of support for the Labour leader were also reported around the time of the second leadership election, with a YouGov poll showing Corbyn winning the backing of 67 per cent of women compared to 57 per cent of men.

Corbyn's anti-austerity stance is often quoted as an explanation for such levels of support – something that is hardly unsurprising given that the House of Commons library predicts that 86 per cent of cuts between 2010 and 2016 have affected women. Many of the young women I spoke to highlighted this as the main reason for their backing of the Labour leader. Abi Jones, a 19-year-old apprentice hairdresser from Swansea, told me that Corbyn's call to bring the apprenticeship wage in line with the national living wage was hugely important in galvanising her support. Jade Wilkes, a 22-year-old postgraduate student, told me that the Labour leader's charge against the 'abhorrent' Tory child tax credit 'rape clause' – a clause which limits tax credits to two children with an exemption for women who have conceived as a result of rape, so long as they fill out a form to state so – sealed her vote. Fran Best, an 18-year-old student of Politics, Philosophy and Economics at Oxford University, told me: 'The manifesto was a proposal for greater social justice and, consequently, improvements to the conditions of young women was rightfully addressed.' Though Fran notes the importance of policy positions, she also told me how Corbyn's campaign style helped to win over young women such as herself:

This campaign felt less like a testosterone-fuelled bid to claim Westminster power and was instead more of an open and inclusive conversation about what we want our society to look like. Campaigning deviated from the working-class men's club environment of old and was re-invented on new platforms. Corbyn addressed thousands of young men and women, from musical festival stages to wide-reaching social media campaigns. Thus, politics was opened up to those typically neglected from the intense inner circle of political campaigning (such as young women) and instead, everyone's opinion mattered.

In the lead-up to the election, my constituency party was joined by Angela Rayner while campaigning on the doorsteps. I didn't expect to find it so refreshing to speak to a fellow working-class woman with a 'normal accent'. Labour's shadow cabinet doesn't just represent privileged white women – it speaks to a diverse array of women from all socio-economic and educational backgrounds. This, paired with the diversified campaigning methods, led to an inclusive atmosphere that had been previously missing from election campaigning.

The different style that Corbyn brought to the election was something that some believed would hinder his ambitions. A young woman who volunteered on both of Jeremy Corbyn's leadership campaigns told me: 'I never believed that he would be able to present a genuine challenge to a structure that exists to keep the very issues he campaigned on – in regards to women – from ever being properly heard, never mind addressed.'

There was, of course, a well-known moment on the campaign trail in May where Rachael Maskell – the MP for York Central – found that the PA system being used during a rally was not quite good enough. Corbyn was pictured holding a speaker aloft into the air, with many young people taking to Twitter to note that the Labour leader was literally attempting to amplify women's voices. Olivia Smith, a retail worker from Brighton, told me that 'young women voted for Jeremy because he was the best listener' and when I told Olivia I believed this to be one of the many reasons people connected with the Labour leader she told me that it was 'particularly true of why young women, sick of being told what to do by men, voted for him'.

Corbyn's support for institutional change has also been noted many times. Writing during the 2016 leadership election for Labour List, Georgie Robertson argued that Corbyn's internal pledges were also important:

Within the party, the new pledges include a Women's Advisory Board and an annual decision-making women's conference to ensure that women are at the heart of policies and decision-making. Labour will also publish a regular 'gender audit' of the Party's policies, and aim for 50:50 representation in Parliament and across all public offices, using gender balanced and all-women shortlists.

Despite all the polling and anecdotal evidence, the youth turnout figures were questioned by a number of sources – another example of young voices being undermined. But it's important to remember that a similar backlash occurred during the EU referendum, when establishment figures rushed to stamp on the idea that more young people had decided to get involved. Research released by the London School of Economics later demonstrated that young people had actually got involved on the same scale as the earlier estimations released immediately after the vote. Yet another survey conducted by YouGov after 8 June 2017 suggested that around 66 per cent of 18- and 19-year-olds voted Labour, with a similar amount of voters under the age of thirty coming out in support of Corbyn.

One of those commentators who questioned the motivations behind the youth vote surge radically changing the British political landscape was Conservative MEP and pundit Daniel Hannan. He declared in the *Washington Examiner* on the day of the election result that 'Young Brits vote[d] for free stuff'. Journalist Tom Welsh wrote in the *Daily Telegraph* on the same day that 'the young are deluded about Jeremy Corbyn, and about much else besides', before adding that 'the Left will continue its resurgence so long as too many go to university'.

The argument became all the more heated after the results were in, with Hannan writing for the ConservativeHome website that 'sooner or later, you run out of spending other people's money ... And young people will foot the bill.' Patronising. Demeaning. Scaremongering. Everything the Tory Party had ever been towards the young came streaming out as they considered Labour's election turnaround. Clare Foges wrote under the headline: 'Let's stop treating the young as political sages' in the *Telegraph* that 'we should be challenging the naïve, unaffordable views of many under-25s, not kowtowing to them'. In short, she seemed to believe that the response to a surge in youth engagement should be to tell them they were wrong, rather than find out why they voted as they did. What these voices should have been considering was the fact that nearly half of young people who voted Conservative in 2015 decided to opt for Jeremy Corbyn just two years later.

Some, however, admitted that a change of plan was needed. Conservative MP Greg Hands told members of the lobby: 'I think we do need to improve our offer to young people.' Another Tory minister said that May 'never even tried' to engage with the young. What this proves is that the youth surge has not just bolstered Jeremy Corbyn, but it has also moved to expose cracks inside the Conservative Party.

As the right failed to understand what was happening with young people, the Labour Party enjoyed as much support offline as they did online. Young Labour members were asking their friends to join them on the campaign and were finding that many were saying yes rather than groaning. For the first time in my life, I was being asked when I would be out campaigning and if people could join me. Some even did so on the morning shift of the election, delivering leaflets as early as 5.30am. Corbyn had made politics cool again. Gone were the days when politics was a dirty word in conversations with young people. Many young people were now desperate to get involved in any way that they could.

One of the untold stories of the election campaign was not just that an incredible number of young people came out to vote, but that an immense number of 18–24-year-olds campaigned explicitly for the Labour Party, both physically and virtually. It was a story of deep engagement that went beyond turning up at the ballot box, and it was perhaps more important for the future of British politics than the surge itself.

Hidden below the extraordinary turnout figures for those aged 18–24 was the fact that many went further than simply just voting. What is so encouraging about this political earthquake is that young people decided to actively engage with the political system in a way that had never been seen before. Fran Best told me that she had also taken the time to get engaged beyond the ballot box: 'I took part in door knocking, local campaign videos for my MP and leafletting. I shared supportive content on all my social media in the months leading up to the election.'

Whether it was traditional physical campaigning methods or online tactics, the young involved themselves at the centre of political campaigning. Where fears were once understandable concerning a lack of youth engagement, this recent general election showed that young people are more interested – and more engaged – with politics than ever before.

This election wasn't just about the younger generation deciding to go out and vote, there was a clear engagement with the wider political process that can only be good for overall democracy, as well as for the Labour Party itself. James Kenney, an 18-year-old Labour supporter, told me this election was 'the first time I ever took part in a political campaign. I knocked on doors, delivered hundreds of leaflets and campaign material and spent ages in the campaign HQ phoning voters.'

James Rafferty told me a similar story:

I didn't vote, being sixteen, but I certainly campaigned hard in the last election. Convincing friends and family members who can vote to vote Labour, tweeting constantly about Labour and why it's important to vote, no matter who you do vote for, getting teachers and school staff to vote. My aim was never to force people to vote Labour, just to get them to vote, and I would make Labour's case.

The Absolute Boy

The perceived wisdom of those operating within the Westminster bubble has always been that young people don't vote and that they simply cannot be bothered with politics. It is why, every time I appeared to discuss political matters on any news outlet, it was usually to be asked patronising questions concerning the political engagement of my own generation.

'Just one more question to you, Liam – you're obviously a Corbyn fan – *honestly* does he have a chance of winning this election . . .?' asked Sky News. 'I genuinely believe that Jeremy Corbyn has every chance, going into this election, of coming out as prime minister,' I replied, as the rest of those in the studio tried to hide their smirks. An LBC interviewer asked me a similar question. 'You don't *really* think he could win, do you?' – as if my belief in Corbyn's vision had been some elaborate scheme to make a name for myself.

Though fascinated by the rise in political interest across my generation, nobody in the media or the political establishment was particularly concerned with taking it seriously. And so the 2017 general election results, and the undeniable Labour surge, came as a surprise to the mainstream punditry. Perhaps this was to a degree understandable: when the polls before the campaign regularly showed Corbyn's leadership ratings plummeting ever further into irrelevance, non-political friends of mine would ask how this matched the massive crowds that would greet Corbyn wherever he would go. As mentioned previously, the answer provided by the press was that it was simply the 'faithful' turning out to welcome their 'dear leader'. Comparisons were made with the big crowds that Michael Foot had addressed, and the apparent uselessness of protesting and gathering to champion an issue, after Foot suffered such a heavy defeat to Margaret Thatcher.

The truth was somewhat different. Corbyn's rallies weren't simply addressing the faithful; many of those who attended were not even members of the Labour Party. Whether it was their physical presence at the events themselves that inspired them to get involved, or the way that videos of the events would spur on support online, these rallies made a real impact throughout Corbyn's leadership and the general election campaign itself. The key to understanding his bubbling appeal was asking why it was that thousands of people were turning out to listen to him speak.

Corbyn's popularity stemmed from the creation of a new

base of support and his appeal was also hugely organic. A number of surprising figures and movements found themselves rallying to Labour's side to register young people and to utilise their engagement for good. There is no better example of this than the way that the grime scene rallied behind the Labour leader and gave political encouragement to a generation of young people who felt entirely detached from a political system that had left them behind.

Whether it was the actual Grime4Corbyn movement or the individual efforts of artists such as JME or Stormzy, figures from the grime scene took the initiative when it came to rallying young people. There was little intervention here from the leader's office. Though some in Corbyn's team were actively reaching out to famous figures, many simply came forward themselves.

Corbyn's comfortable manner with grime artist JME was seen as somewhat of a joke by the media. To some extent it is possible to understand why it all seemed like a bit of a laugh. On one hand you had the teetotal, socialist vegetarian and on the other you had very popular young MCs. But somehow, they came to be strong allies. The truth is that this should not have come as a surprise at all. When Stormzy originally endorsed Jeremy Corbyn, he said he did so because 'he gets what the ethnic minorities are going through and the homeless and the working class'. Young MC Novelist wrote a powerful essay on the importance of voting in *PUSH* magazine just ahead of the general election, where he argued:

First things first. You can't avoid the system. No one can avoid the system. You're not avoiding the system if you choose not to vote, you're still a part of it whether you like it or not. I don't look at politics like a separate part of life. I look at it in the same way I view going to the shops. It's something that we all have to be involved in . . . You can't avoid politics by opting out; it doesn't work like that. We don't have the means to start a new society, we need to control where we're from. We need to try to influence it for the betterment of the people, rather than for the sake of the richest 1 per cent.

What Novelist was saying was no different from the lyrics that he writes. He made clear that he was 'an advocate for Jeremy Corbyn because he is an advocate for that same message . . . I know that Corbyn possesses a sense of decency that I rarely see in politicians'. This is exactly the connection that most young people talk of when they explain why they support him. And that is why the backing of the grime movement was so important: in facilitating this political discussion, young people were approached on their own terms. Grime continues to address the concerns of young people in the post-recession world through words and lyrics, offering a powerful account of the current political situation in a way that is often somewhat hidden. JME of BBK was one of the first to sit down and talk with Jeremy Corbyn, but the support offered from Stormzy, Novelist and AJ Tracey was just as important. At every step of this election, young people found new ways to become engaged. In many instances, it was other young people leading this charge in encouraging their peers.

It is a new base that was on display at Labour's 2017 conference in Brighton. As Tom Peck wrote in the *Independent*:

'There is no point pretending that the Labour leader is anything other than the bona fide, legitimate voice of the nation's youth.' Peck noted that Corbyn's audience at the pre-conference rally comprised 'normal kids, having a normal Saturday night out, sitting about drinking beer and cider out of cans, waiting for a flicker of "Seven Nation Army" so they could chant their very, very unlikely hero's name'. In typical fashion, Peck's article does go on to suggest that it is a shame people have picked a 'political messiah' who is 'unable to convince anyone with a vague understanding of, say, economics, or defence, or general public policy, that he is the answer to the many, many problems at hand'. Corbyn convinced nearly 13 million people of that very fact.

Along with this, 129 economists signed a letter to the *Guardian* ahead of the election stating that Labour's manifesto 'could be just what the economy needs'. While true that Corbyn does not have the support of military chiefs – a hardly unsurprising fact – many of the rank-and-file seem happy with his promise to never sacrifice their lives in vain. Despite accepting that something is happening with the younger generation, many commentators still seem to refuse that it means something, or that it will last. Fired up and more energetic than ever, there is every reason to believe that Labour's new young support base will continue to revolutionise British politics despite the doubts of the naysayers.

A Politics of Hope

Despite the establishment media continuing to support the tactical genius of Theresa May's decision to call a general election, some started wondering whether the prime minister had been wise to make such a move at a time when the country sought some form of direction after the Brexit vote. To many it seemed as if May was putting party ahead of country. When she was elected Conservative leader, the media reaction was almost united in its belief that Labour's end was nigh, as she appeared to be a steady leader at a time when Labour looked divided. Even Tony Blair told an interviewer that he, somewhat unsurprisingly, 'agrees with a lot she says'. May's arrival was seen as worrying for Labour because Corbyn seemed such a risk to many people, whereas May apparently exuded stability and the status quo.

I wrote the opposite in the *New Statesman* when May became prime minister:

> With Theresa May's promotion to prime minister, it is clear that the Labour Party needs the policies and principles of Jeremy Corbyn more than ever. Stripped of the centre-left rhetoric and moral façade, May's platform is one of division. While the country craves unity, it is being offered the same old unworkable solutions to growing problems. The political arena looks more distant from the lives of normal people than ever before. Whether it is the selection of a new prime minister by 60 per cent of a parliamentary party or the lynch mob chasing after Corbyn, the public face of UK politics has been seriously discredited.

Jeremy Corbyn's optimistic message and Labour's general election campaign would turn around all of this doom about the party's prospects. Though there had been a growing acceptance that election campaigns change nothing, and that the results have been decided long before votes are even cast, this recent election would appear to have altered that logic.

Sebastian Payne's election round-up in the *Financial Times* with thirty days to go was written under the headline 'A Campaign Where Nothing Matters'. James Kirkup wrote in the *Spectator*, under the headline 'What Journalists Know, But Can Never Admit: Election Campaigns Don't Matter', that 'what happens on the campaign trail stays on the campaign trail'. Such opinions were based on the polls in many recent elections, but this way of thinking removed the agency of individual voters from the democratic process and, again, patronised people as nothing more than cogs in a machine. Just as young people rushed to claim their ballot, they also surged to reject this idea. The view that the campaign would not be important was allied with the idea that Theresa May was untouchably popular and had showed tactical genius for refusing to partake in television debates. How wrong this opinion would prove to be.

The Labour leader's ambition to win the argument was central to challenging the idea of the 'Corbyn Cult', that his support was all down to his personality. The fact that he was so focused on policy and the argument helped many supporters believe that he wasn't simply in it for himself and that this smear was simply another unfounded attack by the right-wing media. Though comparisons between Donald Trump and Jeremy Corbyn are not helpful for either politician, and often arrived at by jumping to a number of conclusions, it is true that both were able to embolden their supporters in their belief in them while offering to shake up the political system. The morning after Trump's shock victory, I wrote the following in the *Independent* out of the belief that it was the challenge to the status quo that would boost politicians from now on, whether from the left or right:

> And if there's one thing that we can learn from the unexpected result on Tuesday night it is that Jeremy Corbyn can win here in the UK. This is not about left and right, as such; it is about a willingness to stand up to the status quo and call for a genuine change in the way we do politics. That is what Nigel Farage was doing when he campaigned for a change in our relationship with the European Union and for standing up to political elites – and he won the argument over Brexit. From a different perspective, it is also what Jeremy Corbyn is doing. And he can win the argument too.

Corbyn's enabling mentality opened the door to a generation who had been forced out of politics by a class more interested in filling their own cup than standing up for young people. As Sarah Huxley told me: 'For the first time in my life, I had a potential prime minister who cared about the issues me, my family and my peers were facing.'

As young people appreciated the fact that Jeremy Corbyn understood their concerns, the political class continued to peddle the idea that he had no idea what was going on and was somehow isolated in the special world of Islington Labour thinking. One of the most ludicrous misapprehensions that occurred during his leadership was the idea that croissants are some form of delicacy enjoyed only in darkened cafés in north London. Lord Watts, former chairman of the Parliamentary Labour Party, was one of them, criticising those who supported Corbyn's 'disastrous' new politics and suggesting they should stop sitting around in their '£1 million mansions eating their croissants at breakfast'.

Aside from the fact that you can buy four croissants for 69p at Aldi, this whole analogy exposed the extent to which attacks on Corbyn and his supporters were unrestricted, not to mention petty. I have spent a lot of time – too much time – trying to understand what Watts was alluding to here. If it was that croissants are a luxury enjoyed only by the super-rich, he has clearly become detached from reality. But given that Lord Watts is an extremely intelligent man, I suppose that he did this more out of a belief that the 'poor folk' whom his party was supposed to represent may find something strange about this French word, which could make Corbyn seem a bit alien to them.

Watts even used his maiden speech in the Lords to lecture the Labour leadership on what working people need. The irony of this is not lost on us – for a sitting member of the House of Lords to lecture about working people is certainly bold. 'It's their job, and their responsibility, to come forward with policies which will help us to win the next general election. For those who don't want to take on that task, can I suggest they join a society in which they can enjoy sitting around having a philosophical debate about the meaning of socialism,' blasted Watts. It would seem, given Labour's success, that Corbyn doesn't have the appetite for croissants but he certainly has one for exceeding expectations.

In Corbyn, young people found an unlikely wingman

who was more than willing to lend a hand and help them out. A 68-year-old man at the time of the 2017 general election, the Labour leader was well known by then for his love of homemade jam and for keeping his allotment in good shape, often in rather striking and edgy tracksuits. He seemed a far cry from the hip, slick and charismatic politicians that young people are supposedly meant to gravitate towards. Though he certainly did not have the polished delivery of Tony Blair, or the smooth swagger of Barack Obama, this unlikely figure won the political attention of the young through something much more impressive: sincerity.

He may not have looked how a 'young person's politician' was supposed to, but he certainly listened like one should to the concerns of the younger generation. Corbyn's firmly held belief in the importance of listening and learning from other people is often used by the right to attack him as living a life of 'well-meaning mediocrity'. What some fail to understand is that his fundamentally approachable nature is what made him such an attractive figure for the downtrodden young. He was even ridiculed for his underwhelming A-Level grades and academic achievements by the likes of Tory mouthpiece Toby Young, who simply believed that Jeremy was stupid. 'In terms of IQ, Jeremy Corbyn's must be at least two standard deviations lower than his immediate predecessor, and Diane Abbott and John McDonnell are scarcely frontbench material,' he commented in the *Spectator* early in 2017.

But Corbyn's ordinariness was actually one of his most appealing attributes. He wasn't great at the polished politics we had become accustomed to. But who wanted him to be? In many ways, it was his marked difference to the smooth performances of Tony Blair that made him such an attractive proposition: everything about the Labour leader seemed to ooze of the idea that this was not politics as usual, that something very different was happening. There was nothing fake about his unashamed interest in the way that the young were getting a raw deal. His genuine belief that he could change this was a central point around which the early registration drive in 2017 concentrated. People felt as if they had a champion who was prepared to actively engage with them. He quickly became the prism through which Labour's radical message was openly received by my generation.

Corbyn's appeal among the young was no new trend, however. It began long before the drive to register new, younger voters and, indeed, long before the general election campaign itself. James Kenney, an 18-year-old first-time voter, told me that it was during the first leadership election that Corbyn picked up the support of the young. 'I saw Burnham, Cooper and Kendall as just another set of bland Labour centrists with scripted soundbites and stage-managed positions that could be chopped and changed at any opportunity,' he told me, before adding that 'then Corbyn came into the race and I saw someone who held principles'.

Time and time again, young people tell me of the importance of this very point. Corbyn's appeal among the young can be explained, in part, by his commitment to progressive values and his unwavering support for principled positions. For my generation, discovering that he was arrested outside the South African embassy in 1984 for protesting the apartheid regime while the Conservative Party debated whether or not Nelson Mandela was a terrorist was a significant marker of his politics. Discovering that he did not just vociferously oppose the disastrous recent wars in Iraq and Afghanistan, but was also campaigning against British weapon sales to Saddam Hussein in the 1970s and 1980s was also critical. His unwavering anti-racist and pro-equality credentials proved that, despite his age, he was a politician of today who mirrored the collective consciousness of young people.

These points were not necessarily important in isolation when it came to convincing today's young that he was the right choice for them. Instead, they spoke to the wider scope of what he stood for: primarily, what is fair and just. This feeling was echoed in the words of Jonathan Cooke, a 23-year-old Masters student at the University of Sheffield, who told me how 'Corbyn offered something different to what every other political leader was offering at the time and seemed to offer an idea that we should invest in ourselves and some modicum of hope for the future'. This view was repeated by almost every young person that I have spoken to. 'I think I, like many people, felt quite disillusioned with what was on offer in the 2015 election ... Corbyn represented a chance to vote for an alternative vision,' Peter Jackson told me.

And so, from the moment that Corbyn's name was confirmed on the ballot paper for Labour's leadership election in 2015, young people found a champion who they rewarded with their unwavering support. As both Jonathan and Peter suggest, prior to Corbyn's nomination being confirmed, this first leadership election was seen as an inward-looking contest in which every candidate seemed almost exactly the same, despite Andy Burnham pitching himself as the radical candidate. But Burnham's middling approach only helped to highlight Corbyn's genuinely radical credentials. What Corbyn's run invited was an explosion of political activity among the young. Perhaps at this stage it was just those who already had some idea of politics, but it was an explosion nonetheless, with thousands and thousands of young people joining the Labour Party – and reversing a historic trend of declining party membership numbers – to support his passionate alternative. As Rhiannon Lucy Cosslett wrote in the *New Statesman* in the July ahead of Corbyn's first leadership election in 2015:

> It's been reported that a significant portion of the support Corbyn is receiving is coming from new, young Labour members. People like me, who are too young to remember the unelectable eighties, or indeed what 'a comfort zone of Labour politics' feels like. This certainly seemed to be the case at the Islington North meeting I attended last week, where people of all ages, but notably young people, stood up in support of Corbyn. And, despite what his opponents might say, it's clear he has a support base outside of Islington.

Two years after Jeremy Corbyn's humble leadership campaign had delivered a massive blow to the Labour Party establishment, the Labour leader would engage the young once again to deliver a similar blow to the British establishment itself. There is a point behind seemingly trivial polls, such as that conducted by the university news network The Tab, which found, just a month ahead of the election, that 'over 80 per cent of young people would rather go on a night out with

Jeremy Corbyn than Theresa May'. At the same time The Tab asked this question, thousands of students were seen at an outdoor rally in Leeds, climbing trees and lampposts to get a glimpse of him. A friend who was there, after patiently waiting for hours to see the Labour leader, told me that it was 'like nothing I had ever seen before . . . students just took over the whole of Oxford Road and closed it down, nobody was leaving until Jeremy Corbyn had spoken'.

And while this singularity of young people finding a best friend and hero in a 68-year-old bloke makes it all the more interesting, age is clearly not everything. Corbyn was able to convince young people that he cared about the issues that affected them. This point about 'caring' is particularly poignant to the people I spoke to in the last few months. Isra Shamal noted that there was a draw to Labour owing to the fact that you 'can really tell that Jeremy Corbyn cares about the people', specifically saying that 'you can see his care and interest for us . . . he represents our views and has our interests at heart'. His commitment to the offer of honesty and hope chimed with a generation fed up with self-serving politicians.

As one of the respondents told me:

I supported Jeremy, and continue to do so, because he offers hope. Hope to our generation who have little prospect of buying a home, hope to those who are fighting for an end to the 1 per cent pay cap, hope for those who are having to work zero-hour contracts and are being exploited by their employers because of it . . . Only Jeremy understands the plight of our generation because he actually engages with us.

As Jeremy Corbyn's perceived support from the younger generation was confirmed, the response to this was further ridicule. Instead of trying to understand why this has happened, the Conservative Party has concocted all sorts of magical explanations. Many believe that this is just a one-off. Some Conservative cabinet members have taken to believing that the failure of history lessons in British schools to educate young people about the atrocities of Soviet communism rests as an explanation for his support among the young. The scramble to understand what has happened has further exemplified just how disconnected our political class really is from the population it seeks to serve.

Chapter 4

THE RESPONSE

OUTCLASSED

In wider society it has become popular to blame the young –
or 'millennials' – for anything and everything. In 2016,
millennials were blamed for 'the vanishing bar of soap', for
falling 'out of love with diamonds' and for 'killing the napkin
industry'. The media loves a good story that focuses on bash-
ing young people and young voices. The *Atlantic* went as far
as to publish an article with the headline: 'How Millennials
(Almost) Killed the Wine Cork'.

As funny as much of this is, it is also depressing. It has
become entirely acceptable to make sweeping generali-
sations about the young as the idle murderers of a better
world. The stereotypes are damaging and counterproduc-
tive. They ensure that young people remain locked out or
disengaged with whatever industry chooses to side against
them. In politics, this has been no different. Because of
policies such as the triple lock on pensions, much of the cost

of austerity has been levelled on the backs of the young. Though the poorer older generation have felt the impact of austerity, many have been protected by such promises. Given that money and resources cannot be cut from these areas, it has instead been taken from the young. I am not proposing that the old be robbed in order to support the young. Instead, this government should get serious about tackling tax evasion and corruption so that all of our people can be provided for, whether young or old.

The Tory attack on Corbyn's tuition-fee pledge was just another example of blaming young people, in this case for wanting a better and fairer future. Sadly, even when the young welcomed the call to be engaged and involved, they remained marginalised. These sentiments, however, are the dying call of an ideology and belief system that will find itself sliding into irrelevance if it doesn't seek to understand what is behind this phenomenon.

It was BBC presenter Andrew Neil – no friend of the left by any means – who put it most incisively when he asked a Tory MP why the young should believe in capitalism when they cannot accrue any capital, with house prices so high and so many coming into the workplace burdened with student debt. And yet, rather than tackle this question with any intellectual curiosity, most of those on the right believe they can save themselves by ramping up the rhetoric around the idle young and attacking them further. For this, they will pay an ultimate price in terms of electoral politics. Since the election, numerous polls have demonstrated that young people continue to flock towards the Labour Party: a YouGov poll in November 2017 showed that the Conservative Party were down 7 per cent in terms of their support from the under-30s, from 22 per cent to just 15 per cent.

Clutching at straws, the British establishment moved to create their own narrative. Shortly after the final result of the election was announced, a poisonous and false assumption spread. Corbyn's success, it was claimed, was down to the fact that people voted for him only with the comfort of knowing that the Labour Party would lose the election. The claim was based on little – if any – evidence, and could not have been further from the truth.

Statistical evidence – not based on conversations had over plush dinners in Westminster, where these fantastical notions are usually formed – shows that people were more likely to vote for Labour in constituencies where they believed they could win. As Jon Mellon and Chris Prosser – the researchers behind the 2017 British Election Study Internet Panel – put it: 'The more likely someone thought Labour was to win a majority, the more likely they were to vote Labour.'

This isn't to say that everybody who voted Labour did so expecting a victory, but such a nuance was often lost. When this new smear spread, it was as if everybody had voted for Labour in the belief they would be nowhere near power, so they were 'safe' to do so in the knowledge that none of it would actually happen and they were just reining in May's majority. Perhaps those of us on the left should stop affording these commentators such leeway. It wasn't only the right who made this argument. Labour MP Joan Ryan encouraged voters to vote for her 'whatever your misgivings about the Labour leadership', while Tony Blair argued that people voted for Corbyn out of a determination to 'neuter the mandate'. Labour MP Ruth Cadbury told voters that she could only help remove Corbyn if she was re-elected.

Even when the evidence was clear for all to see, it didn't stop some from claiming that it was all somehow fake. When a triumphant Jeremy Corbyn took to the stage at Glastonbury in front of a crowd of hundreds of thousands of people – most of them young – the usual 'hot takes' were produced. Apparently, he was addressing the middle-class intelligent-sia, rather than generating mass support. How could it be otherwise at a festival that cost over £350 for a ticket? After all, poor young people are clearly more interested in buying tinnies than they are saving up to go to a festival that may be the highlight of their year.

Ipsos MORI found that Corbyn's support with the young crossed all class lines. The poorest of the young, those in the DE class category, supported the Labour Party with 70 per cent of the vote. The C2 class backed Labour with 62 per cent of the vote. Among the C1 class, 58 per cent of these voters went for Labour. Even in the richest bracket, the AB class, 52 per cent supported Labour. Every class of young person backed Corbyn's message of hope and optimism. So, while the media attempted to play divide and rule with young people, the truth was that his popularity among them ran across the board. Though there are constant attempts to simultaneously define Corbyn as a croissant-eating member of the Islington elite while also saying that he failed to convince high earners of his unashamedly left-wing message, the truth is more straightforward: Jeremy Corbyn and his politics are immensely popular with the young. Whether rich or poor, young people were willing to listen to the man who had taken the time to listen to them.

Given that the result surprised so many, there was plenty of research done into what persuaded people to vote for Labour. Polling by YouGov, conducted in the month after the general election, found that the main reason people voted Labour was down to support for the party's manifesto and policies (28 per cent of people cited this as their main motivation), while 15 per cent noted their vote was anti-Tory in nature, and 13 per cent of Labour voters noted Jeremy Corbyn as the main reason for their vote. YouGov noted that 'the Corbyn effect is very much in evidence within the results'.

The polling agency also noted that 'while overall 13 per cent of Labour voters say that Corbyn was the main reason they cast their ballot for the party, this rose to 24 per cent among 18–24-year-olds'. Such a statistic clearly demonstrates the level of support that he commands across this new base. This chimes with YouGov polling released directly after the 2017 general election which stated that 66 per cent of 18–19-year-olds voted Labour and 62 per cent of 20–24-year-olds did the same. YouGov headlined this research by noting: 'Age is the new key predictor of voting intention in British politics.'

NatCen has also conducted interesting research on who voted for the Labour Party in 2017. The research organisation notes:

One point is clear. Labour was relatively successful at winning the support of those who did not vote in 2015. Just over a quarter (27 per cent) of our panel members who did not vote in 2015 turned out and voted Labour this time. Labour's gains from this source were responsible for some four in ten of the votes that it gained as compared with 2015. In contrast, the Conservatives won the support of only one in ten of those who abstained in 2015, and indeed these were too few to counterbalance those who turned out for David Cameron two years ago but stayed at home this time around.

NatCen also divided their panel into six different classes. Of these six classes were two younger groups, the 'Young, disaffected JAMs' and the 'Liberal Youth'. The first group are defined as 'Younger working-class voters with mixed views whose main distinguishing characteristic is that half did not vote in 2015'. The second group are defined as 'mostly younger people in middle-level non-graduate jobs though they have yet to get on to the housing ladder and tend to think of themselves as working class. They are, however, relatively liberal and positive about immigration.'

The research group found that the Labour Party surged by fourteen points among the 'Liberal Youth' and twelve points among the 'Young, disaffected JAMs'. Peter Kellner noted in the *New Statesman* that 'altogether, 10 million of the 30 million people who voted in 2015 either changed party or abstained this year'. Labour's base is changing on a massive scale, both in terms of welcoming new supporters and also those who left the party over New Labour.

As the Conservative Party struggled to come to terms with Labour's election result, Corbyn seized on it as an opportunity to rally young people further. He called it the victory of the young. Paul Flynn, the veteran Labour MP, dedicated much of his victory speech to the 'welling up' of young people who had been politicised by 'hope, idealism, integrity'. Labour's massive lead among all classes of young people was welcomed by a host of Labour MPs, with some in marginal seats devoting their victory speeches to those inspired by his message.

THE GREAT BRIBERY?

The other central negative narrative of the election remains that young people were 'bribed' by Jeremy Corbyn over the promise to scrap university tuition fees. A projection, perhaps, as for decades, the Conservative Party has mastered this game, offering the older generation anything and everything to keep them on side. Whether detrimental to the national economy or to the prospects of the young, the Conservatives have arguably 'bribed' the old at every single general election before 2017. In reality there is little difference between an offer and a bribe – it is kind of what elections exist for. The Conservative Party made a conscious decision, however, to characterise Corbyn's offer to the young as a 'bribe', because it helped them to discredit his claim to be serious about making life easier for today's young. But, as Theresa May found, it is hard to win the votes of people if you opt to offer them absolutely nothing.

This idea that Corbyn offered a 'bribe' to the young in the form of free education is just wrong when it comes to understanding why young people voted the way they did. While it is true that the Labour Party promised to ensure that all those due to start university in September 2017 would be free from paying the fees, most of the young vote that turned out for Corbyn did so in the awareness that they themselves would not benefit from Labour's policy.

Take myself, for instance. I have graduated from the London School of Economics with £27,000 worth of tuition-fee debt – excluding the maintenance loan cost. But I was just as excited about Labour's policy on abolishing tuition fees as my youngest sister, who would benefit from it. The difference between us wasn't the belief in the policy, but rather the fact that I could actually vote. Those who were already attending university voted for Labour in massive numbers, just like those who have recently graduated. There was no 'bribe' for those of us who had graduated, other than the fact that we wanted the next generation to be free from the burden that we had faced. The high cost of university education forces the fortunate to rely on the 'Bank of Mum and Dad' and the less fortunate to seek multiple insecure and low-paying jobs alongside a full-time university degree so as to be able to afford to attend. The only bribe was the comfort of knowing that a fairer platform within the university system was on the table.

This was warped in the weeks following the election in further fantastical stories purporting to explain the rise in young Labour voters. On the return to Parliament, an idea took hold in the press that those of us who voted for Corbyn had been betrayed. The betrayal was down to the fact that he had supposedly promised during the campaign to abolish all historical tuition-fee debt, from those who started paying the fees at the very beginning on the lesser rate to those of us saddled with £27,000 worth of student debt. Now he was saying that Labour would not abolish all historic student debt after all.

There is no evidence to suggest that Labour ever made this promise. A few Labour figures appealed to the aspiration of alleviating the debt that young people were facing. Corbyn himself told *NME* magazine that he was keen to look at issues such as the interest paid on the loans and the threshold at which repayment began. He did, however, caution that he had no 'simple answer'. Personally, I believe that when he said 'I'll deal with it', he meant it. In context, the interviewer was asking about the plight that young people face carrying this burden of debt. In reality, it is a tax that comes out of your pay packet each month, meaning you have less money to spend on transport, food or even entertainment. Corbyn's manifesto addressed much of these issues along with student debt. Labour's entire promise was to 'deal with' the crippling cost of normal life for people.

But, as usual, what he actually said didn't matter in the eyes of his opponents and the mainstream media. Conservative backbenchers rose in the Commons to demand an apology from the Labour leader over the 'lie' that had been sold to millions of voters. Iain Duncan Smith even went as far as to say that Corbyn had used the young as 'election fodder'. Once again, the Conservative Party found itself buying into the idea that young people were easily led and naïve, prone to making rash decisions simply because they were promised the earth. YouGov polling completely dismissed this view. It found that just 16 per cent of 18–24-year-olds had believed the Tory smear that Corbyn would abolish all historical debt. The vast majority of young voters unsurprisingly took Labour's pledge to abolish tuition fees from September 2017 as a pledge to abolish tuition fees from September 2017.

Another malign idea developed in the wake of the election was that the young had 'double voted'. 'This many young people simply could not have come out to vote' appeared to be the view of the British establishment. The justification for this allegation came from the fact that students are able to register at both their home address and their university address (in order to vote in local council elections). It was then utilised as a weapon, suggesting that young people had corrupted the system and voted twice in the general election. From the Conservative point of view, it appeared that the support of the young for Jeremy Corbyn was either down to naivety or electoral fraud.

After trebling tuition fees, scrapping the Education Maintenance Allowance and removing housing benefits from 18–21-year-olds, the Conservatives had shown themselves completely incapable of understanding what it means to be an average young person today. The fact they hadn't realised it reveals a wider failure of their grassroots movement and highlights why the Conservative Party will always struggle to win over young people in the same way that Corbyn did in the 2017 general election. There seems to be an embedded attitude on the right towards the young, one that dismisses their concerns and issues.

Nevertheless, some in the party realised that the election highlighted a problem. The existence of Activate is proof of the fact that some Conservatives are aware that something must be done to engage young people within the political process. It is hard to welcome this, given that we now know the underlying views of those attempting to inspire right-wing youth engagement. Our concern has to be the fact that the Conservative Party seems to accept the need to win more young votes while also doing very little to appeal to them in any serious way as regards to policy. They will certainly have a lot of money to throw at any organisation that establishes itself to target young votes. It remains less certain if it could ever be successful, given that it would be launched purely with the cynical aim of getting those votes in a ballot box, rather than the moral reason of securing a better future for the young people that bother to get involved with any party within our political process.

There seems to be some form of awkwardness that appears whenever Conservatives attempt to entice the young. Whereas Corbyn's popularity was achieved without gimmicks, through a genuine interest in listening to young voices, the Tory Party has come up with some patronising promises to the young since the general election. The right-wing think tank Adam Smith Institute released a twelve-point 'Millennial Manifesto' that served only to prove the gap between those on the right and young people. The organisation argued that the Conservative vote would 'soar' among young people if they cut air passenger duty for the under-30s, noting that the tax should be dubbed the 'Ibiza tax'. Labour's Shadow Minister for Voter Engagement and Youth Affairs, Cat Smith, noted that 'this is a laughable failure to understand what young people care about'. Quite.

Other parts of the paper also sounded surreal, for example the passage on recreational drugs: 'Many young people take recreational drugs. Occasionally some of them smoke a cannabis spliff with friends. Many of them pop an ecstasy tablet to help them enjoy late-night dancing at a club. Some of them try amphetamines or snort a line of cocaine.'

Any young person that bothered to read such a passage

would know that this was not serious political engagement. Who calls a spliff a 'cannabis spliff'? Who calls clubbing 'late-night dancing'? Nobody, that's who. These attempts to understand young people and to engage with them are embarrassing. It may just be that the wrong people on the right are attempting to prevent the disconnection with the young. But for as long as reports such as these are released and young people continue to feel patronised, the right will have no chance of engaging in any meaningful dialogue with the young.

This failure reached all the way to the top of the party. On the eve of the Conservative Party conference, the prime minister announced her long-awaited pitch to young voters. The right-wing press did its best to paint May's reforms as revolutionary. The *Sunday Express* splashed: 'That's More Like It Mrs May' as they explained the prime minister's pledge to 'overhaul tuition fees'. The *Sunday Telegraph* called the pledge 'May's Fees Revolution' after the prime minister announced her plan exclusively to a paper well-known for its youthful audience. You can just see it now: groups of young people rushing to the newsagents to pick up their copy of the *Sunday Telegraph* to read about May's revolution. The *Mail on Sunday* joined in the excitement, and noted 'May's Audacious Bid for Youth Vote' as the plan found its way to the front pages.

So what had they done? After Corbyn's pledge to scrap tuition fees was so well received, was the prime minister pledging to go further and scrap all existing debt? No. The revolutionary pitch promoted by the Conservative Party was to freeze tuition fees at £9,250, just a few weeks after they'd hiked them by another £250. The next top-up of £250 was to be 'scrapped' – or, more likely, delayed. The Conservative Party also announced that students will not have to start repaying the loan until they are earning at least £25,000, but delaying repayment does nothing to address the fact that it will still have to be paid. Advancing the argument that some people will never have to pay it back does little to support the Conservative obsession with reducing the national debt.

Allowing the student debt budget to build ever higher will only create a crisis within the university system at some point in the future. The announcement was a short-sighted one, as it failed to address the real issue for students. Furthermore, it will also cause a headache for the government who introduced a 'teaching excellence framework' in the last parliament to award universities with the best standards the ability to raise fees. On the issues of appealing to the young and education reform, it is clear that the party is in absolute chaos. The adoption of Corbyn-lite politics suggests that they have given the 'raving Marxists' in charge of the Labour Party some power within their own ranks.

This feeble attempt shows just how out of touch Theresa May really is. What will survive is the Conservative ignorance as to what actually needs to be done. The party could have made a point of the fact that the middle classes would benefit from free tuition fees, but instead they have ignored this point and attempted to 'look good' on the issue. In this sense they have forfeited the argument entirely. The Conservative Party clearly feels that it can promise anything on fees, however small, and with a bit of good publicity claim huge credit. They have failed to understand what has happened and what really inspires the young. We are young, not stupid. But the Conservative Party seems keen to continue with its condescending tone when it comes to addressing our legitimate concerns.

At a time when British politics seems to be becoming more divided on the demographic of age, kicking the issue of tuition fees into the long grass seems like a silly strategy for the Conservative Party. Polls show that Labour continues to struggle with securing the votes of the older generation, despite offering real policies to them. If Labour cannot get hold of older votes, despite offering to protect the pensions triple lock, free bus passes and the winter fuel allowance, it seems unlikely the Conservative Party will gain any younger votes by offering nothing substantial. Indeed, a number of young people said as much to the *Guardian* in response to the announcement.

Ruby Dalziel, twenty, told the paper that the announcement on tuition fees was of 'no interest to me whatsoever because the Tories lie and have done consistently. There is no reason for me to trust them. It's an attempt to win votes and I won't be swayed – Jeremy Corbyn all the way!' Carmen Kirkby, also twenty, helps to explain just how dangerous the position seems for the Tories: 'The Conservatives could not do anything that would change my mind and make me vote for them. They are a horrible party for breeding fake values.' Ash Camyab, eighteen, helped to support the idea that students won't be fooled by window dressing, telling the paper: 'The Tory government isn't actually helping students, they just want to be able to say that they are. Labour is actually trying to make a genuine difference.'

The Tories also sought to address the issue raised by

Andrew Neil: the fact that young people can't afford to get on the property ladder. However, the announcement of an extra £10 billion worth of funding for the Help-to-Buy scheme was an equally ignorant response. An increase in demand is, strangely enough, not what the housing crisis needs. The current problem is down to a lack of supply: there is not enough affordable housing for young people to buy. This headline-grabbing initiative was supposed to shore up the image of the Conservative Party as being on the side of the aspirational young, but the reaction to it suggests just how large the paradigm shift has been within British politics. It even resulted in Andrew Marr asking the prime minister how she was going to pay for these pledges – a question normally reserved for Labour politicians only.

The idea of a radically socialist British government no longer seems such a crazy one. With every passing day of Conservative chaos, it becomes ever more likely that Jeremy Corbyn will be carried into Downing Street on a wave of support from the betrayed young across our country. It is no longer a question of 'if' Jeremy Corbyn – or indeed his platform – could be elected, but rather a matter of when. That is why it is so important that our political leaders understand what this new wave of support was built upon.

THE MOMENTUM

Once referred to as 'a rabble' by deputy Labour leader Tom Watson, Momentum helped to inspire young people to become engaged with the political process. Just as Corbyn was denigrated by the Conservative Party, so too was this young and energetic group that was established to support Corbyn's leadership of the Labour Party – and not just by the Tories. One area where the Conservative Party was particularly worried by the power of this grassroots organisation was revealed in a leaked briefing delivered to *The Times* on 2 July. It demonstrated the frustration felt by Conservative MPs, who believed that they were 'massively outgunned' when it came to social media. It is rumoured that the party is now planning to quadruple its social media team and to invest heavily in social media output. Essentially, this is a case of imitation being the sincerest form of flattery – despite the fact that the imitation looks set to be a very poor one.

Clearly suffering from some serious fear of missing out, an online Conservative grassroots campaign reared its ugly head under the name of 'Moggmentum' shortly after the general election. Billed as a movement 'celebrating Jacob Rees-Mogg in a similar fashion to the 2015 phenomenon of Milifandom', the group even has its own Wikipedia entry. While 'Moggmentum' was a fairly innocent – and admittedly somewhat funny – online campaign, the launch of 'Activate' by young Conservative activists turned out to be something altogether more sinister. The Activate group lists its aims on its website: 'Engage young people with conservatism, showing them what centre-right politics can offer'; 'Provide a platform for young Conservatives, facilitating the discussion of issues that matter to young people'; and 'Foster links with Conservative University and Constituency Associations, encouraging members to become involved with the Party & influence policy'.

These seem like pretty normal aims, but, as with all

attempts to engage young people by the right, this one burned out within a matter of hours. The Activate UK campaign started with a few serious flaws. First, one should never put the phrases '#meme' or '#rt' in a tweet given that this both looks ugly and breaks every rule of social media. Second, don't name your Twitter handle with two underscores. These are just basic issues that demonstrate a deeper misunderstanding of young people from supporters of a party that is locked in the past. A browse of the 'People' section of their website – which was quickly taken down – showed the organisation to be made up of a handful of male Conservative students being told what to do by old hands from the larger Conservative establishment.

And though it is easy to laugh at the fact that the Conservative Party believes it can overturn a record of anti-youth politics and policies with a meme, what was released in the days following Activate's launch exposed the true face of young Tories. WhatsApp threads, which had been leaked, named 'professional discussion board' – and apparently contained some of those establishing the Activate group – showed young Conservative activists joking about 'gassing chavs' and 'shooting peasants'. In true Nazi-inspired rhetoric, one activist called for 'medical experiments' to be conducted on the working classes, with another adding that 'we could use them as substitutes for animals when testing'.

A spokesperson for Activate said that none of the comments came from anybody serving on their – now defunct – national committee. The Conservative Party also distanced themselves from the group, saying that 'Activate are in no way affiliated with the Conservative Party'. Denying affiliation is one thing, but we wait to see whether any official outreach plan will do any better. My suggestion would be for people not to hold their breath in anticipation of this. The current low levels of support that the right has received from the young will continue until the Conservative Party recognises that it has a real duty to address the growing concerns of young people. It can offer slogans and platitudes as often as it likes, but a failure to offer any concrete policies that tackle ever-increasing inequality will lead only to their own demise.

Meanwhile, Jeremy Corbyn is inspiring his party to make that happen with a series of eye-catching, imaginative policies across a range of issues that are fundamentally important to young people.

PART TWO

What Next?

Chapter 5

OUR FUTURE

MOVING ON

The growth in turnout and active participation among the young at the 2017 general election will not continue unless they remain engaged and involved in the wider political process. It will take hard work and clear thinking for this involvement to continue to grow. For the Labour Party to further cement its appeal with young people, it must be braver and bolder than ever before and cannot become complacent, feeling that the job is done. Just as William Beveridge established a plan to tackle the five giant evils of his day, politicians must be brave enough to create a policy platform with young people's interests at its centre. It is a staggering stain on our current society, and an indictment of the political class's ignorance that my generation is currently predicted to be the first to do worse than the one that came before it.

To reverse this trend – and to quite literally save the future – the Labour Party must not be afraid to flip the table and cast aside the dogmatic traditional rules of the old politics. The party must challenge the very core of a political system that has been constructed in a way that enables it easily to ignore and dismiss marginalised voices, such as those of the young, whether it be the patronising way in which we are usually approached or the fact that 16- and 17-year-olds continue to be denied the vote. When I was fourteen, a campaign that I launched in Lincoln on this very issue received some press coverage after I wrote to David Cameron demanding that 16- and 17-year-olds be given the vote, owing to the fact that they could sleep with their MP but not vote for them. The local press doorstepped my granddad and asked him whether he would support the measure as a former politician; his reply was: 'Liam has a way of putting things that makes it hard to disagree with him.' Perhaps this was the first sign of agreement between the young and old!

There are both structural and policy debates that need to be held for such a change to occur and for young people to believe that they are actually listened to. As a senior aide within Jeremy Corbyn's office told me: 'There are still millions of young people who are either not registered to vote or who are but didn't vote in June 2017. So we have to keep going on a voter registration drive – and keep engaging with colleges, universities and through social media. Trade unions also have a role to play in recruiting and organising young people at work.' It is refreshing that those in the Labour leader's office are already thinking about how they can attract more young people, rather than simply accepting the current level of engagement as enough. With millions of them left to bring in from the cold, it is important that we respect and celebrate how far we have come while also refusing to lapse into complacency.

Though radical proposals on policy and structural changes will be key, the root of Corbyn's appeal – the willingness to engage openly and honestly with the concerns of the young – must remain the centrepiece of any political commitment to my generation. But it must go further and deeper than him alone. To the delight of his opponents and the worry of his supporters, he will not be the leader of the Labour Party for ever. This is why it is so important that our engagement must find a concrete and lasting base. Our future seems to rely on his popularity and his personal respect for our concerns, which help drive the team around him.

But that could all change in a matter of moments. Though the political future looks positive for Corbyn and the Labour Party, if the 2017 general election taught us anything it was that foregone conclusions can fail to materialise. Our political future cannot rest on one man alone. The real test of his support for the young will be whether he can bring about deep and lasting change in terms of reforming attitudes towards my generation. His legacy could be more than just this amazing rise in youth engagement. Though what happened at the 2017 general election has already transformed British politics, if kept alive it has the potential to transform British society.

Having sparked a revolution of sorts, it is now our duty to carry it forward. We must find a way to carve Corbyn's concern for the young into the fabric of British society so that the problems we face are viewed as top priorities rather than easily dismissed issues. My generation knows that our loyalty cannot be blind to any leader or any party. If we are given reason to challenge the party if it is not working in our interest, we should. But we have not been given good cause to do so, yet. Some have suggested that it is on the issue of Brexit that Corbyn faces a potential challenge from the young, and this is something that will be discussed later within the wider context of what the Leave and Remain campaigns represented in 2016. Now that the political establishment is aware of this growing coalition of young voters, we must not be afraid to demand more than we ever have before – from both the Labour Party and wider society.

For too long we have been told to accept that which we are given, to be content with the way that society works, even though we are fully aware of the fact that it is not working – especially not for us. As a generation that emerged into the world as adults in the post-crisis era, we are fully aware of the unfairness and the inequality that grips our society. We are desperate to change this, to forge a future where things are fairer and more equal, and where believing in such a society and fighting for it is not laughed off as utopian or unachievable.

We answered Corbyn's call from 2015 when he told us that we didn't have to take what we were given, that we could aspire for more. And we did. We must make our political movement more accessible and we must invest more in our political system so that we can change it for the better. Some of this work will be dull and boring. Sadly, it will not all be a reflection of the energy and the enthusiasm that was felt in the crowd at Glastonbury or the celebration that we all saw at Prenton Park when young people chanted 'Oh, Jeremy Corbyn' and sparked the beginning of the wider interest in our youth surge. The hard, detailed work of changing politics so that we can change the country is hardly as enticing as attending these rallies or events. But it is the only way that we will achieve lasting change in our society to build on our achievements at the 2017 general election. We now have a duty to constantly consider what more we can do to cement our position as a force to be reckoned with within the British political system. The 2017 election cannot be another one-night stand for progress in the Labour Party.

One of the reasons I wanted to write this book was not simply to look back at what has happened, but as an attempt to bring our movement together, to take stock of what we have achieved so far and to chart a path for the future. Having spoken to thousands of young people about what it is that we can do to keep engagement levels as high as they are – and to push them even higher – I believe that there are a number of things that we can start fighting for today that will pave the way for our engagement to become a constant occurrence at every single general election. None of this is simply what I alone believe – this analysis and this manifesto of sorts have been deeply informed by conversations with the wider movement and with young people across this country. We must now demand the change that we wish to see in our society, and then fight for our own new deal.

It won't be simple. The result of decades of political apathy among the young has been the wholesale dismissal of our concerns. When young people have asked for more, we have been knocked back. Our support networks have been cut to the bone and we have been accused of whinging when we have complained that things are simply not good enough.

Labour are the only party truly listening. The main reason

that the Conservative Party will continue to struggle when it comes to engaging with young voters remains the fact that they refuse to have any serious conversation with us on policy. After years of ignoring the plight of young people, the Conservative Party has suddenly become much more interested in getting our support. Though Downing Street and Conservative HQ will continue to brief that they take the concerns of young people seriously, their fascination with promoting gimmicks at the expense of any meaningful consideration of the issues facing us will only serve to confound rather than convince. They don't really want to hear what we have to say; instead they want to persuade us why their way is going to benefit us.

Instead, young people are crying out for a fundamental change in the way that society works. The Tories have completely failed to understand that this is what rests at the root of Corbyn's popularity among the young. This failure was clear in the first Labour leadership election and again in the general election, when commentators attempted to analyse the youth surge. There appears to be some sort of paralysis within the British establishment which has been left confused and dazed by a response they just can't understand.

Theresa May and senior Conservatives appear to believe that the Labour leader's popularity is based on his ability to be 'down with the kids'. Such thinking has been found in Conservative strategy before: how can we forget David Cameron's disastrous 'hug a hoodie' approach? But what the prime minister, the Conservative Party and the media continue to miss is the fact that Labour's newfound resurgence – particularly among the young – has more to do with

'Corbynism' than it does Jeremy Corbyn. As we have seen, it was the policy direction of Labour's 2017 general election manifesto that excited young people more than the personality of its leader. Though the manifesto was eloquently professed by the Labour leader throughout the election, it was the ideas and concepts within the document itself that captured the hearts and minds of young people.

Any party that wishes to be taken seriously by the younger generation needs to offer proper solutions to the problems that we continue to face in our society. That means proposing radical new solutions – not gimmicks – to issues, whether it be addressing the mental healthcare crisis within our National Health Service, tackling the haphazard approach to Brexit negotiations, dealing with the chronic lack of affordable housing in this country, raising the issue of insecure jobs and low pay, or coping with the eye-watering cost of receiving an education.

Though there have been significant detachments between the generations throughout history, the gap has never seemed as wide as it is today. Despite this, young people share the same concerns as their elders and the wider society of which they are a part. We spend money in the same shops as everyone else, we use the same public transport as everyone else and we use the same public services as everyone else. We are not different in the way that we engage with the world around us. It is therefore unsurprising that young people are not solely concerned with issues that most directly affect us and cannot be won over simply by being offered a bung here or there on tuition fees.

There is, of course, a 'young' element to the big issues.

But overall, unsurprisingly, young people care about the same things that most other people care about. In a survey conducted by ICM, they overwhelmingly cited the crisis within the National Health Service as the most important issue influencing their vote in the 2017 general election. Brexit was a somewhat distant second consideration, but still came ahead of education and tuition fees – the questions young people are expected to care about more than anything else. This survey provides useful evidence that they did not become involved in the 2017 general election because they wanted handouts and gimmicks.

What is clear is that young people backed Labour in greater numbers than ever before because they believed that the party had the right answers to the questions of our time. This belief has continued to manifest itself in the aftermath of the general election. A YouGov poll released in late August 2017 revealed a massive divide in the trust that they placed in both parties on the major issues. The poll found a huge lead for the Labour Party among 18–24-year-olds, with headline voting intention standing at a staggering 66 per cent for Labour and a shockingly low 14 per cent for the Conservatives. These figures are almost an exact opposite to the support that is enjoyed by both parties with the oldest generation.

The reason for such a gap was revealed by more specific questions in this YouGov poll. Among young people, 52 per cent believed that Labour is best placed to manage the National Health Service, while just 6 per cent backed the Conservatives. On housing, the Labour Party is trusted to tackle the current crisis by 44 per cent of young people, with just 4 per cent of my generation trusting the Conservative Party to do the same. On the issue of education, Labour is seen as best by 48 per cent compared with 9 per cent for the Conservatives.

Even on the issue of Brexit, where the Labour Party receives little positive press, young people back them by 29 per cent, with just 10 per cent believing that the government is best placed to negotiate Britain's exit from the European Union. Though this is not a ringing endorsement for either political party – given that most don't know – it is telling that young people prefer Labour's Brexit vision over the Tory one. What it all highlights is that the support for the Labour leader among the young is rooted in a belief that Labour's radical policy platform will deliver the change that they so desperately crave in a society that they believe is becoming more unfair and more unequal than it already is.

The Labour Party has already offered young people something of a new deal in its 2017 general election manifesto. When compared with the Conservative Party manifesto – which was devoid of ideas and offered very little to any generation, never mind the young – Labour's platform was seen by its supporters as a real antidote to our broken society. But there is, as always, more that can be done. Indeed, Jeremy Corbyn himself admitted that Labour's manifesto was put together quickly owing to the snap nature of the election. Embedded within such an admission is that fact that the Labour leader perhaps believes that he can go further. While he might have been constrained by a parliamentary party anxious about going into the general election with too radical a manifesto, the 2017 result may just allow him to enter the next one on an even more radical platform. It is clear that more can always be done to inspire young people and engage them in the political process, and that is our next challenge, which I want to focus on for the rest of the book.

As the Conservative Party scrambles to establish some sort of offer for young people, the Labour Party finds itself in the fortunate position of already having large support from them with the time to develop a strategy to attract even more. It seems that the Labour Party will enjoy doing so, with the Conservative Party struggling as it attempts to forge its offer to the young. In September 2017, Chancellor of the Exchequer Philip Hammond told his backbenchers that the government must do more to alleviate the difficult economic position young people across the United Kingdom continue to find themselves trapped in.

According to one Conservative MP, Hammond contrasted the plight of young people with his own position, telling the Conservative 1922 Backbench Committee that his generation had 'no mortgage . . . a pension and . . . more money in the current account'. It is hard to take the chancellor's concern for the young seriously, even if you argue that Hammond was simply highlighting the disparity between the generations. But you cannot absolve him of his previous failure to do anything about the crisis young people face. One would suggest that some humility would go a long way when it comes to any Conservative outreach programme that the party should attempt.

Theresa May's hint that the Conservative Party may review the formula by which graduate loan interest rates are calculated simply proves how rattled the establishment is.

Even though May touted this idea to the press, it was quickly dropped. Downing Street has rushed out all manner of briefings, from reducing tuition fees to 'naming and shaming' those institutions which overcharge while falling behind on teaching standards. It is important to note here that whatever policy the government comes up with – which will be known by the time this book is published – will fall short of the expectations of the young. Unfortunately for the prime minister, these moves will be seen as nothing more than panicked and ill-thought-out attempts to outmanoeuvre the Labour Party on the issue of tuition fees.

The fact that the prime minister believes her problem with young voters can be solved with a stand-alone pledge to lessen the burden of tuition-fee debt demonstrates just how out of touch her government is when it comes to their concerns. In failing to address any other area of the lives of young people, the Conservative Party appears to simply be scrambling for votes, rather than advancing any genuine concern or interest in the unfortunate state that the majority of young people find themselves in in modern Britain. Whether university students, apprentices or full-time employees, attempts to woo young people with the odd policy here and there will not do enough to reverse the entrenched belief that conservatism and capitalism continue to fail those doing their best to get by. A lack of interest in other issues that impact young people will only push more towards what is now an attractive socialist mode of thinking.

As young people become more radical in their political thinking and engagement, it is likely that the Conservative Party will only become more and more desperate in their attempts to attract their support. The party has so far failed to inspire any real belief that they care about young people, instead opting to try to win votes with terrible memes and ill-judged humour. The truth is that young people will only engage with the Conservative Party on the basis that they offer the hope of a better future than the one we currently find ourselves living in.

Perhaps the reason Labour is better at convincing young people of this rests with the fact that they have lived through seven years of Conservative leadership. Over that time, we have seen living standards fall and our own financial situations worsen, with HSBC figures demonstrating that 18-30-year-olds continue to see their monthly disposable income falling. A report by the Resolution Foundation in 2016 found that the current young generation earned a significant £8,000 less during their twenties than their parents in Generation X.

Whether the Conservative Party is willing to make such a concession is yet to be seen. In reviewing the policy areas that young people care about, it becomes more obvious that Conservative ideology is in direct opposition to the changes that young people want to see. This is the real problem, then, for the Conservative Party. Not only are their leaders and representatives seen as distant from the young of today, but their entire ideology is seen as alien.

A Mental Health Crisis

Taking the time to analyse the current crisis in mental healthcare through a political lens helps to explain why young people backed Labour in such large numbers. For as long as the Conservatives continue to offer warm words but little action on the issue, it is unlikely they will find themselves on the receiving end of youth support. Only politicians who are open about this issue and who can present a plan to fund these services will be taken seriously. The health of our people should be one of the greatest concerns of government. It certainly is for young people.

It is unsurprising that young people continue to report that the state of the National Health Service remains their number one political priority, as was seen in the 2017 general election. Though the wider crisis in the NHS – such as an increase in waiting times and a lack of GP services – is certainly an issue for young people, it is the underfunding of mental healthcare provision that seems to cause a genuine anger among the younger generation.

This was certainly the case with many of those I consulted when I wanted to understand why the NHS was so important to them. In nearly every conversation, the young people I spoke to would talk about mental health in particular, often about an event that had impacted them personally relating to either their own mental health or that of a family member or close friend.

The UK's most senior family judge, Sir James Munby, stated in August 2017 that he was 'ashamed and embarrassed' by the chronic lack of mental healthcare provision in our country. Sir James was commenting after a case in which no hospital bed could be found for a 17-year-old who was deemed at acute risk of suicide after previously attempting to take their own life. Stories of young people forced into prison cells, owing to a lack of hospital beds for mental health patients, are all too regular in today's news cycle, demonstrating that the state of mental healthcare provision in this country remains disgraceful and wholly inadequate. Sir James warned that this case was just one of many and that the country would have blood on its hands given the serious lack of mental health support currently available for young people.

Though mental health problems can affect people of any age, it is well documented that there is a disproportionate number of young people suffering from mental illness. A recent report by the Institute for Public Policy Research demonstrated the seriousness of this growing crisis, with the number of students admitting to suffering from a mental health problem upon registering at university having increased by 500 per cent since 2007. National data covering 60 per cent of NHS mental health trusts across England shows that some 250,000 children receive regular mental healthcare – and this figure includes only the documented cases, never mind those who are suffering in silence or unable to access the care services that they need. As such, the number of young people suffering in this way is likely to be much higher than the official figures stated.

The generally accepted statistic that one in ten young people suffers from a mental health problem may well be somewhat outdated, given that it was reported in February 2016 that the rates of depression and anxiety in young people have ballooned by over 70 per cent over the past quarter of a century. In all areas of life, professionals continue to report a staggering rise in young people suffering with mental health issues. A Parent Zone survey in 2016 found that 93 per cent of teachers admitted to seeing increased rates of mental illness among their pupils, with 20 per cent of teachers saying that they had to deal with a mental health-related problem in the classroom on a weekly or daily basis.

Health professionals in the NHS continue to talk of the strain that has been placed on mental health provision given the continued underfunding of the service itself. Without the funds that these professionals need to deliver the service so many young people evidently require, there is little room for improvement on the current situation. When health professionals are standing alongside young people calling out for more support, it is clear that politicians must get their act together and do something to adequately address this growing crisis that receives little media attention despite having such an impact not just on the health of young people, but also on their wider wellbeing and trust in society.

It is no surprise that this situation has become politicised. Given that young people rely on these services more than ever, as levels of depression and anxiety continue to rise, they are rightly asking why they cannot receive the care they need. They continue to call out for parity between the way mental and non-mental illness are treated. By this they mean they want to ensure that mental healthcare receives the same amount of financial support and resources as physical health, so that access to mental healthcare is just as readily available. This has been a demand for some time, but it was given heightened prominence in this recent general election, where the issue of mental healthcare featured more prominently than in previous campaigns.

And there was a marked difference between the two party leaders on the issue. Though both Theresa May and Jeremy Corbyn spoke openly about the growing mental health crisis among young people, it was the Labour leader who came across as more genuine and who was able to hold the respect of young people on the issue. He spoke to *Kerrang!* magazine during the election campaign about attending the funeral of a 16-year-old girl in his constituency who had tragically taken her own life. He used this experience as a way to rally against the chronic underfunding of mental healthcare provision in the country while noting his own engagement with a number of voluntary mental health charities. It was, after all, under his leadership that the position of shadow mental health minister was created and elevated into the shadow cabinet for the first time, before the role was scrapped after Labour MPs mounted a leadership challenge against him in the summer of 2016. This showed the seriousness of Corbyn's concern. His history and proven track record in championing greater access to mental healthcare seemed at odds with the prime minister's warm words, which had less to back them up.

To be fair to May, she did continue to call for a shake-up of mental health policy during the 2017 general election, having gone as far as to promise a revolution in the way that the issue is addressed. She even used her first speech as prime minister on the steps of Downing Street to address the mental health crisis in the country, demonstrating the importance that she placed on it. Behind the rhetoric rests a record, though.

Sadly, the Conservative record on the issue of mental healthcare fails to match young people's demands for mental health reform. Though the prime minister spoke of recognising parity between mental and physical health, the country has not seen this vision transform into reality after more than seven years of Conservative leadership and over a year of her at the helm. Over the previous parliament, funding for mental healthcare fell by 8 per cent and there are as many as 7,000 fewer mental health nurses compared to the number in 2010. Stories of young people having to travel hundreds of miles to receive care, often detached from their family and friends, have received prominence in the national media and have become all too frequent.

Theresa May could not even bring herself to match the pledge she made on the steps of Downing Street within her own election manifesto, which signalled a retreat from her promise to recruit a total of 10,000 new mental health nurses. The Conservative manifesto only went as far as to promise that 'up to' that number would be recruited and the decision to allow for such wiggle room on this subject damaged the sincerity she had previously given the issue. The worry regarding this subtle change was well founded, given that the 2015 Conservative manifesto had promised to increase funding for mental healthcare, whereas it soon became apparent that between 2015 and 2016, Cameron's government actually oversaw a cut in funding for 40 per cent of mental health trusts. May's decision to water down her promise was a real warning to people who were suspicious about the difference between what politicians do and say. At a time when young people were calling out for honesty in the political arena, May appeared to believe she could get away with what seemed like underhand tactics.

Though young people consistently seem more concerned

with mental health provision than their elders, this gap is narrowing. Labour's manifesto offered real policies to tackle the mental health crisis, along with Corbyn's seemingly intuitive understanding of the problems that people faced. The manifesto promised to properly ring-fence mental health budgets to protect services; it vowed to use prisons only as a place for serious offences and to initiate a review of mental health services in prisons; it noted its plan to end the 'scandal' of young children being treated on adult mental health wards, promising to end 'out-of-area' placements whereby families are often detached from one another owing to a lack of services near where they live. When it came to young people specifically, Labour's manifesto promised to increase the proportion of the mental health budget that is spent on young people as well as introducing school-based counselling services for all schools.

Though any one young person may not have suffered with, or be suffering with, a mental health problem of their own, it is likely that they will know someone who is. Given the serious and chronic underfunding of the NHS since 2010, it is wholly unsurprising that this issue has rightly become a politicised one within this age group, and beyond. Young people are all too aware of the impact that politically motivated cuts continue to have on these health services, which they might at some point seek to access, in many of the same ways the rest of the country does.

In some respects, it is this issue that really unites young and older people alike. Young people, familiar with grandparents suffering awful care conditions or long hospital waits, did what they could to back the party most trusted to improve the condition of the National Health Service. And the older generation also came out in support of their children and grandchildren, who they may have assisted through mental health crises of their own. There didn't seem to be any sense of the 'Hunger Games' playing out between the generations; each generation wanted the help to be available to all. Labour's message unashamedly told the country that these services could receive the funding they needed, without slashing the benefits enjoyed by the old for the benefit of the young.

BREXIT BRITAIN

Since David Cameron offered the nation a vote on whether or not to stay in the EU, it is hard to have a political discussion on any topic in the UK without eventually bringing up the question of Brexit. Every area of political life seems to be touched by the issue, with our exit from the European Union hanging like a cloud over any discussion of the future, given how important it is that we get it right. The popular vote to exit the European Union continues to confound commentators and politicians alike, irrespective of which side they backed.

Throughout the referendum campaign, much was said about young people offering their overwhelming support to the Remain camp, because this was seen as the more progressive argument versus a regressive one that was often deployed by the Leave side. The truth is that the referendum was flawed from the moment that it was called. Cameron had calculated that the vote would heal an age-old divide on Europe within the Conservative Party, and so he made the basis of the referendum as wide as it possibly could be. The question that was asked on the ballot paper – 'Should the United Kingdom remain a member of the European Union or leave the European Union?' – was worded in that way out of arrogance and delusion.

So sure was Cameron that the country would vote to remain in the EU that he never considered that the vagueness of this question would come back to haunt politicians of all persuasions. Some argue that the question could not have been simpler, and this is true. But the problem with our exit from the European Union was that it was never going to be simple, and that what it meant to 'leave' the EU was open to different interpretations, so if the unthinkable happened, there was no clear next step. Had he thought there was a real danger of voting for leave, he might have tried to define the term more closely.

Whatever anybody thinks of the decision taken in June 2016, it is undeniable that the country voted to leave the European Union. At the root of the serious question being asked now regarding the country's relationship with the EU is not necessarily whether the UK should or should not leave the institution, but rather how it does and on what basis the future relationship operates. It is, again, unsurprising that young people should note Brexit as one of the most important issues influencing their vote in the 2017 general election, given that it will continue to dominate the political landscape, with the result of negotiations dictating the future for many young voters.

A recent Ipsos MORI poll conducted for the British Council found that more than two-thirds of young people in the United Kingdom said they had an 'international outlook' – one can assume that this means young people feel more connected to the wider world than ever before, with information now readily available on crises facing distant countries as well as our own – with many registering their fears regarding British withdrawal from the European Union. Interestingly, the report found that a majority of young people (57 per cent) were positive about the effects of globalisation, suggesting that its development is seen as a good thing among the young.

The point that is relevant to this book, then, is why on earth young people who are apparently passionate about the European Union, concerned about Brexit and positive about the concept of globalisation would back a well-known Eurosceptic who has rallied against globalisation his entire political career? At the centre of the current Brexit debate – particularly concerning the attitude of the young – is this logical inconsistency between the international outlook of young people and their apparent support for the European Union and their overwhelming backing of Corbyn.

Jeremy Corbyn is a Eurosceptic. The Labour leader voted 'No' to membership of the European Community in the referendum of 1975 and voted against the creation of the single market in 1986 and also voted against the Maastricht Treaty as well as the Lisbon Treaty. In an article in 2009, he stated that 'the project has always been to create a huge free-market Europe, with ever-limiting powers for national parliaments and an increasingly powerful common foreign and security policy'. In other words, Corbyn's euroscepticism was in line with the typical left-wing opinion of the EU as an anti-democratic institution.

Socialist journal *Jacobin* summed up left-wing opposition to the project during the referendum campaign in an article where an author noted that 'the European Union provides internationalism for the bosses, not the workers'. This has long been a feeling across the left. They have always seen the European Union as an anti-democratic institution that exists to protect the privilege and interest of the capitalist class. True socialists note that the European Union has existed as a vehicle for economic and cultural neoliberalism, with many arguing that its pummelling of the Greek government during the financial crisis confirmed this once and for all.

Yanis Varoufakis, former Greek finance minister, argued that Greece had been placed under a 'postmodern occupation' by a neoliberal order intent on hollowing out Greek democracy and society. This is a position that Corbyn's close circle would have agreed with at the time – indeed, the Labour leader often attended rallies and demonstrations in solidarity with the Greek people. Despite some media commentators arguing that he has attempted to hide his Euroscepticism, it is somewhat unfair to suggest that the Labour leader has not been open about his opposition to the free-market forces that operate within the European Union.

In what some leftists saw as a betrayal, Corbyn campaigned for the Remain side during the European referendum. He called for the British people to accept the current state of play, endorsing the European Union 'warts and all'. Why? Surely his opponents are right to note that the Labour leader, so often seen as a man of unwavering principles, betrayed his own convictions and is not worthy of the praise heaped on him for his habit of standing firm, even when the majority of opinion goes against him? Not quite.

Though attacked for an apparently 'half-hearted' defence of the European Union, the Labour leader deserves some credit for the position that he took. In the metropolitan bubble – where our journalists and commentators reside – a doting love for the European Union may be entirely normal, but it certainly is not for the country at large. Most people shrugged their shoulders during the European referendum, including myself. I called on the left to back Remain in a similar vein to Jeremy Corbyn, more out of a fear of a hard-right Tory-controlled exit than a love for the institution itself. I spoke to many young people who admitted to doing the same – many campaigned within the 'Another European is Possible' group, which attempted to bring these voices together. We will never know the impact of Corbyn's position throughout the referendum, but rather than sinking the Remain campaign, it is my opinion that he probably brought people into it. Sadly, 'remain with reform' was not an option on the ballot paper. Owing to this, the hatred and lies whipped up by the far right and the Leave campaign led to their victory – just.

So why was Jeremy Corbyn's 'half-hearted' support for the Remain cause not the undoing of his leadership, as so many had predicted? Why do young people, so enthused and supportive of the European Union, continue to back the Labour leader in such staggering numbers? It's simple, really. Much of the support for both the European Union and the Remain campaign that came from the young during the referendum was about values, not institutions. Despite its often regressive policies, the institution was seen as a symbol of progressive values. More importantly, the Remain campaign, because it was in opposition to a hard-right Leave campaign, became a beacon of those same values. The young coalesced around the Remain campaign because it projected the values that they believed were fundamental to a decent society.

The initial response to the vote – that young people had been robbed of the opportunity to learn and to love across the Continent – was proof of this romanticised idea of what it meant to be European, or what it meant to be a Remainer. The EU was able to gain this symbolic position, despite the fact that thousands continue to perish at sea on its outer frontier and that working-class Europeans continue to be punished as much by neoliberalism as those at home. Removed from the institutional argument, the referendum campaign – for young people at least – became a fight between what was right and what was wrong, what was good and what was evil.

The values that young people believed were present in the Remain campaign are undoubtedly present within Corbyn's leadership. The 'betrayal' of young people therefore seems to be little more than a smear concocted by commentators as another way to bash the Labour leader. Jonathan Freedland wrote in the *Guardian* that young people were in 'a state of mourning' following the result and that they had been let down and 'betrayed' by the Labour leadership. 'The facts are plain: Corbyn, McDonnell and their inner circle betrayed the hopes of the generation that believed in them most,' he wrote.

Less than a year later, millions of young people rallied behind the Labour leader and delivered the stunning and unexpected result that we saw in the 2017 general election. It seems that the betrayal young people were apparently suffering from was constructed by a largely middle-aged, middle-class clique of journalists who were hurting and scared to admit to their own tears in light of the referendum result.

In the aftermath of the European referendum, YouGov polling has suggested that 49 per cent of 18–24-year-olds either voted to leave the European Union or have accepted the referendum result, in comparison to just 35 per cent who would vote to have the result overturned. The idea that the institutional make-up of the European Union, and Corbyn's support or opposition to this, would be a deal-breaker for young people shows exactly how out of touch such commentators are. Robbed of opportunities, with our voices removed from the political scene and in a world where politics has failed to give us anything we have asked for previously, why would we be surprised that we did not get our own way during the referendum campaign?

Though the debate over Corbyn's Brexit position continues to offer much excitement to the media, these tired arguments are of little concern to the young people that I have spoken to across the country. The hatred of the Leave campaign, and its embodiment of regressive beliefs and values, allowed the Remain camp to become a beacon for all that young people hold dear. The arguably racist and anti-migrant undertones of the Leave campaign repulsed young people and Corbyn's Euroscepticism is very different to that.

Young people do not feel betrayed by the Labour leader, because they know that he represents the values they care about even more than the Remain campaign did during the referendum campaign. In a sense, he is granted a pass on the biggest political issue of the day because young people feel safe in the knowledge that if he was prime minister and in charge of the negotiations, we would be moving towards a progressive exit that both respected the democratic will of the country while also protecting the values that young people stand for. The thing that scared those I spoke to was the fact that the negotiations have been left in the hands of a hard-right Tory clique that is hell-bent on appealing to the worst in people.

The fact that young people continue to support Corbyn despite his Euroscepticism is a proof of this theory. Such a belief is supported by research into the way that the younger generation thinks and feels about social factors in comparison to the older generations. They care more about global issues, such as climate change and human rights, and are far more comfortable with migration than their elders are.

The British Attitudes Survey sheds further light on this point, noting the generational divide on moral and social issues, which helps to explain the way different value-sets aligned with each respective campaign during the European referendum. The obsession with learning about or understanding 'millennials' comes down to realising the fact that it is unsurprising that young people are progressive in their political outlook. In the European referendum, the Leave campaign was anything but progressive and I remain firm in the belief that this factor helps to explain the inconsistency of my generation backing the Remain campaign by a majority while also backing Corbyn.

The only Brexit policy that will appeal to young people

is one that promises to tackle the wider issues that they face in the modern world, while also promising a commitment to a progressive withdrawal, where rights are protected and co-operation on climate change remains intact. That sort of exit from the EU now seems to have more support than overturning the result altogether or holding a second referendum. What is certain is that the Conservative Party's negotiating position is leading us onto the path of a hard-right job-busting Brexit that is definitely not supported by the young. The true betrayal is that of a prime minister who seems keen to crush the futures of young people in securing a Brexit that delivers little for them.

What should be offered to the young on Brexit is a meaningful engagement where their voices are placed at the centre of the British negotiation strategy. The government should have called for public consultations with the young to calm their fears and include them in the process of forging this new future outside of the European Union. We know that this has not happened yet and it is unlikely that it will. If the Conservative Party was serious about engaging young people, the best way to demonstrate the sincerity of this pledge would be to include my generation in the design of our future relationship. Given the prime minister's record, it is highly unlikely that she believes young minds could be trusted with such a major decision. The fact that our future is in the hands of the likes of Boris Johnson and David Davis is the genuine worry for the young, and it is high time that the media paid more attention to this fact rather than the constant smearing of the relationship between the Labour leader's Brexit stance and the younger generation.

A Broken Planet

Bright Blue – a self-described 'independent think tank and pressure group for liberal conservatism' – released a poll in September 2017 to try to gauge what young people were thinking about the major issues of the day. It was also an attempt to understand the way young people judged the Conservative Party on such issues. Many were surprised by the fact that 18-28-year-olds cited climate change as the most important issue when it comes to choosing which party to vote for in a general election. As some Conservative commentators and politicians noted at the time, this is a major problem for their party.

As the report itself notes: 'When under forties were asked to describe their perception of the Conservative Party's current policies on climate change, the most commonly selected adjective was weak.' This is somewhat unsurprising. Despite David Cameron's 'hug a husky' trip to the Arctic in 2006, the Conservative record on climate change is less picturesque than the image of the then opposition leader posing with furry animals with a snowy backdrop. The problem with the Conservative record on the environment is that it has always relied on platitudes and not policy.

Despite talking up the world's first Green Investment Bank at any given opportunity, Cameron later sold it off. His government, and now Theresa May's, continue to embrace fracking while removing subsidies for wind turbines. Cameron took credit for a scheme set up under the Labour Party which saw 99 per cent of the UK's solar capabilities installed while he was prime minister. At the same time, he cut solar incentive programmes by 65 per cent. Even the platitudes changed. Cameron went from promising to be the greenest government ever to reportedly telling aides to 'cut the green crap'. No wonder young people cannot bring themselves to trust the Conservative Party on the issue of climate change.

Theresa May set her position on the environment in stone very early on. Within twenty-four hours of being confirmed as prime minister, she abolished the Department for Energy and Climate Change, moving responsibility for the issue of climate change to the newly established Department for Business, Energy and Industrial Strategy. May also initially made Andrea Leadsom the Secretary of State for Environment, Food and Rural Affairs. As the *Independent* reported at the time: 'Her voting record shows she generally voted against key measures to stop climate change.' The appointment was certainly not a good look for the Conservative Party, to say the least. Leadsom admitted to the All Party Parliamentary Group on Unconventional Gas and Oil in October 2015 that the first question she asked when appointed as a minister at her new department was: 'Is climate change real?'

After the 2017 election, May moved Leadsom on and recalled Michael Gove to the cabinet, making him the new environment secretary. One of Gove's former colleagues, Ed Davey, wrote an extraordinary piece in the *Guardian* condemning the appointment. 'Putting Michael Gove in charge of the Department of the Environment is much like putting a wolf in charge of the chicken coop,' wrote Davey, adding: 'I sat around a cabinet table with Gove, and he couldn't help playing to the Tory climate-sceptic audience.' With a record like this, it remains unsurprising that the Conservative Party fails to engage young people on the issue of climate change.

The concerns regarding climate change are reflected the world over. It is not just young people in the United Kingdom who are worrying about the issue. In a report published by the World Economic Forum, it was found that this remained the biggest global concern for millennials for the third year in a row, with 48.8 per cent noting that climate change and the destruction of nature was the most serious issue affecting the world today. Some 91 per cent of young people surveyed agreed or strongly agreed with the fact that science has proven that humans are responsible for climate change. When you juxtapose the concern that young people in Britain have regarding climate change with that of the wider population, the difference is stark. In January 2016, YouGov found that 'out of seventeen countries surveyed worldwide Britain is among the least concerned about climate change'. The divide on attitudes remains a wide one, with the older generation feeling less concerned about the issues that seem to motivate young people the most.

Theresa May's lacklustre response to Donald Trump's withdrawal from the Paris climate change accord will not have encouraged any young people to take another look at the Conservative Party. At a time when Jeremy Corbyn called Trump's decision 'reckless and dangerous', the prime minister's silence was deafening. Corbyn accused May of a 'dereliction of duty' in failing to sign a statement supported by other EU leaders which called on Trump to reconsider. Labour's manifesto, coupled with Corbyn's personal and longstanding commitment to tackling climate change, addressed the concerns of young people head-on.

Within Labour's energy sector re-nationalisation plan was a promise to enforce climate targets from the heart of government, along with the commitment to ban fracking and put the UK back on track to meet the Paris Agreement targets. The manifesto noted that 'tackling climate change is non-negotiable' and stated that Labour would 'reclaim Britain's leading role in tackling climate change'. The Conservative manifesto boasted of Britain's achievement of being the first nation to introduce a Climate Change Act, omitting that it was introduced by a Labour government and not a Conservative one. With the backdrop of a Conservative record that has failed to deliver, it is no wonder young people trust Corbyn on the environment.

The Conservative Party spent much of the 2017 general election campaign preaching that Corbyn's Labour would return the country to the 18th century. This was despite the fact that the Tory manifesto pledged to hold a vote on the repeal of Labour's ban on foxhunting. Animal welfare has become a major political issue in recent times. In November 2017, the Conservative Party was forced to deny that they did not vote in favour of the idea that animals are not sentient. Tory MPs' offices were flooded with complaints after the Commons voted against transferring the EU protocol on animal sentience to the UK statute book during the passage of the EU (Withdrawal) Bill.

David Bowles, head of public affairs at the RSPA, said that it was 'shocking that MPs have given the thumbs down to incorporating animal sentience into post-Brexit UK law'.

An amendment to the Bill, proposed by Green MP Caroline Lucas, focused on the precise wording of a piece of EU legislation that explicitly described animals as 'sentient beings'. The Tories were accused of voting down legislation that confirmed that animals could 'feel pain'. The response was massive. Rachel Maclean, Tory MP for Redditch, denounced it as 'fake news'. Robert Halfon, MP for Harlow, penned an open letter addressed to 'many' of his constituents which declared his belief that 'animals are sentient beings'. MP after MP rushed to social media to declare their undying support for animals.

Given that support for foxhunting and the ivory trade caused much damage for the Conservatives during the 2017 general election, the party scrambled to respond to the PR disaster online. During the week of the 2017 budget, Downing Street was forced to confront an unfolding story that they did not believe animals could feel pain. A week later, Rowena Mason, deputy political editor at the *Guardian*, reported that Conservative MPs had been 'called in to Downing Street' to discuss the fact that the country views the party as 'compassionless'. As Mason noted, the party had 'been particularly stung in recent weeks by a social media campaign claiming Tory MPs voted against recognising animal sentience' with 'Tory social media accounts ... pumping out video rebuttals stressing that Michael Gove, the environment secretary, is committed to recognising animal sentience in EU law'.

This was largely due to the fact that the government had also been shocked by the response to their pledge of a vote on returning foxhunting and the omission of a promise to ban the ivory trade from the Tory manifesto. It is somewhat unsurprising that young people were less than trusting of a

Conservative Party that has continuously stated its ambition to allow people to dress up in funny clothes and enjoy the tearing of an animal limb from limb to support any meaningful legislation on animal rights.

There is still more that Labour can do to promote the role of young people in the fight against climate change. Though written some years ago, the call by Kazi Ateea – a youth climate change activist at the time and co-signatory of the climate change campaign 'The Future is Ours' – for young people to be given a seat at the table of future UN climate change negotiations is one that should be supported by the Labour leadership. This is another area where young voices are missing from the top of the debate. Rather than being given the chance to lead on the issue that concerns them most, organisations such as the UN seem to talk down to young people.

The appointment of Jayathma Wickramanayake as UN Envoy on Youth – a representative with a history of activism from the age of twenty-one – is a welcome step by the organisation, but it must go further by appointing young voices across the board. Young people are incredibly active and engaged, yet charities and NGOs fail to mobilise us in the same way that Corbyn's movement has done. There is probably some connection between this fact and the failure of 89 per cent of NGOs to employ a full-time or part-time social media executive. At a time when 28 per cent of 18–24-year-olds cite social media as their main news source – outstripping traditional modes of news sources by some margin – global environmental campaigns cannot afford to be lax on this point. The same goes for the Labour leadership here at home.

It is imperative that the example set by Corbyn's 2017 campaign is championed across all left-wing social movements. No issue needs such a champion more than the issue of climate change, especially given that young people are calling for the issue to be given the focus that it rightly deserves.

No Place Like Home

According to data released by the Office for National Statistics, in 1991, 36 per cent of 16–24-year-olds owned their own home. The most recent figures relating to younger home owners are for 2016, where the data shows just 10 per cent of the same age group owned their own home. Although some of this change can be put down to the increasing numbers staying in full-time education beyond sixteen, the rising price of housing is the most important cause. But the trend of falling ownership continues into the next two age groups, from 25–34 and 35–44, making the goal of home ownership appear almost impossibly distant.

Whereas young people have seen their chances of owning a home dashed, the comparative figures for the older generation show the opposite trend: in 1991, 62 per cent of 65–74-year-olds were home owners, whereas 78 per cent are today. There is perhaps no greater statistical comparison that exists to demonstrate why young people feel so aggrieved with the unfairness and inequality that is present in our society today. How on earth is the Conservative Party – and capitalism itself – supposed to survive when the root promise of their ideology is dying out along with their voters? This is a vital issue for the Conservative Party to resolve given the longstanding link between property owners and how they vote; it is no surprise that Theresa May is so desperate to find a way to solve this problem.

One of the key principles of capitalism – and its Conservative Party mouthpiece – is that if you work hard, you will get on. Not just that, but if you work harder than other people in society, you will receive a greater reward for doing so. This is the basis of capitalism. May's concern for the downtrodden 'Just About Managing' class is an acceptance, however, that there is a flaw somewhere within our current model, as the link has been broken.

Nowhere is this flaw more evident than with the current housing crisis that this country faces – one that hits young people harder than most. Young people are working in an increasingly competitive environment. Yet they find themselves unable to take that first step on the property ladder, despite the Conservative Party consistently telling them that they will be able to. Unless one inherits enough money for a deposit and then has a wage far exceeding the national average, it is nearly impossible for a young person to take that step towards buying their own first home, especially in and around London, where average house prices are more than twelve times average salaries. Some do, but they probably do so with the support of parents or grandparents. And even then, they find themselves snowed under with mortgage repayments and are forced to make significant sacrifices elsewhere in their lives. Though this may all seem like a choice that is par for the course, it is a massive decision given that many of their friends may not be able to make that same move and so may end up leaving them behind.

Margaret Thatcher's wish to turn the United Kingdom into a 'home-owning democracy' has turned into something of a pipe dream for many young people today. Our generation, 'generation rent', is now expected to pay a much larger multiple of our earnings than our parents and grandparents did when they first bought a home. Thatcher's plan was supposed not just to afford people the right to buy their homes, but to make them more likely to vote Conservative. It did just that. In many ways, the housing crisis that continues to unfold before us is a product of her disastrous policy, as four out of ten homes sold under Thatcher's right-to-buy programme are now owned by private landlords. *Inside Housing* magazine has dubbed Milton Keynes the 'right-to-buy-to-let capital' of England owing to the fact that over 70 per cent of right-to-buy homes are now owned by private landlords. The policy has both reduced the stock of social housing while also ensuring that this previous stock has ended up in the hands of private landlords who are making a killing out of rent. It should be known as the great housing robbery.

This problem has important political ramifications. Ipsos MORI data released in the weeks following the 2017 general election showed that private renters – a group that is disproportionately made up of young people – opted for the Labour Party in greater numbers than before. In the 2010 general election, the Conservatives had a 5 per cent lead over Labour among this demographic. In 2017, Labour led the Conservatives by 23 per cent among voters who classed themselves as private renters.

Steve Akehurst, head of public affairs at the housing charity Shelter, wrote in *CityMetric* following the election: 'We can say housing – and the impact of the housing crisis on private renters – is one of the key factors that helped polarise results on 8 June.' In pointing out that private renters spend an average of 41 per cent of their salary in rent, while home owners spend just 21 per cent of their salary of their mortgage, Akehurst argues that 'the 2017 election was arguably the moment where the power of Generation Rent was felt for the first time'.

With nearly half of all private renters being aged between sixteen and thirty-four, it is clear that this current housing crisis disproportionately impacts the young. On this measure, it is no surprise that young people were so keen to make their voices heard in the 2017 general election. Denied opportunities in other areas of their lives, the central promise of the Conservative Party to future generations seems to have materialised into nothing other than an unachievable dream for most young people.

I would argue that the housing shortage facing young people today goes much further than the simple comfort of being able to afford to own the roof over your head. Even those earning well above the national average wage are forced into multiple occupancies, with some young families even house-sharing with friends because they simply cannot afford to rent a place of their own, never mind buying a family home.

If you are earning £40,000 a year – roughly £13,000 above the national average annual wage – and working forty hours a week, you feel let down by the fact that you are still having to fight for a shower in the morning. It's not fun, trust me. There was once a belief that the place you lived in was supposed to be something more than a room where you dropped your bag and went to sleep, or that a sofa was for lounging about on and watching TV rather than somewhere to sleep every night.

Sharing a place with an excessive number of people for an excessive price is simply the start of the problem when it comes to housing and it is by no means the worst part of the experience. It is the hours spent arguing with property managers and landlords over broken pipes and leaky windows, which you then most likely end up paying for to be fixed. The housing crisis is about much more than the financial situation that young people find themselves in. It is something that impacts the health and wellbeing of young people up and down this country, especially as so much of what is on offer is poor quality.

In 2016, the Citizens Advice Bureau released a report estimating that private landlords were taking £5.6 billion worth of rent on homes that fail to 'meet legal standards'. They came up with the damning estimation that over 700,000 families in England were living in homes that pose a 'severe' threat to the occupants' health. Shelter estimates that the number of people living in rented accommodation that is unfit for human habitation stands at over 250,000. How can we even claim to live in a civilised society when this is the housing that we give our young people in 2017?

Before even getting to the issue of building more affordable homes, the Conservative Party has failed to protect those forced to rent. In 2016, the Conservative Party voted against a Labour amendment to the Housing and Planning Bill which would have required private landlords to ensure their homes were 'fit for human habitation'. Marcus Jones, the communities minister, said at the time that while he believed homes should be fit for human habitation, they could not pass a law that explicitly required this to be the case. How reassuring.

Prior to the voting surge in the 2017 general election, the Conservatives seemed entirely dismissive of the plight of young people facing problems within the housing market, again offering platitudes in place of actual policy. Their sudden interest since then will be seen as a grubby attempt at vote-grabbing.

What young people will remember instead is the Conservative plan at the beginning of 2017 to strip housing benefit entitlement from single 18–21-year-olds. The policy was first proposed under David Cameron in 2012 and such a long-planned move shows the true instincts of the Conservative Party when it comes to young people and the issue of housing. Kate Webb, head of policy for Shelter at the time, said that it would almost certainly lead to 'an increase in rough sleeping'. The Tory explanation at the time was to ensure 'that young people don't go straight from school and on to a life of benefits'. It is important to remember the deep-rooted history of a party that has never shown an interest in helping struggling young people before, whatever new ideas they come up with.

So what might the alternative be for young people? At a time when wider society is touting 'micro-flats' as the solution for the housing shortage in major cities, it is important that Labour focuses on a real revolution in housing. Let's be honest, 'micro-flats' are the last thing young people need. A micro-flat basically amounts to a home where you sleep on a ledge and have to rest your palm on the oven while you pee. Such 'innovative' plans will continue only to line the pockets of landlords; they are not the answer to this problem and never will be.

The crisis within the housing sector has been brewing for decades. In 2007, the Labour government pledged to build 240,000 homes every year, but this target has never been met. In 2012–13, the nation managed to build only 135,500 new homes, despite claims from a number of housing groups that we needed at least 250,000 per year. Labour must promise to increase supply by letting the state build again. Prior to Thatcher's 1979 election, local councils were building in excess of 100,000 homes per year – sometimes more than the private housing sector. Now, that figure is a tiny fraction of that number, and the private sector has not made up the shortfall.

Just after Labour's disastrous result in the local elections in May 2017, Jeremy Corbyn made clear that his top priority in this area would be to build more social housing and to regulate the private rental sector. Corbyn told the *Guardian* at the time that there would be a specific focus on young people. Labour's 2017 manifesto went some way on this, but the party must go further in addressing the issues young people will face in regards to housing until it has managed to build more homes.

Now that the Labour Party is aware of the popular appeal of Corbyn's radical message, perhaps it will reassess the more radical elements of his leadership campaigns. The one policy that must make the move from the Corbyn camp to mainstream Labour is the plan to extend right-to-buy initiatives to private tenants. It is hard to level the criticism of hesitancy at him, given that he argued for just this radical move during his first leadership campaign:

> We know that Generation Rent faces an uphill struggle simply to get into long-term housing. We have seen some good ideas from Labour to establish more secure tenancies for renters. Now we need to go further and think of new ways to get more people into secure housing. So why not go with Right to Buy, with the same discounts as offered by way of subsidised mortgage rates, but for private tenants and funded by withdrawing the £14 billion tax allowances currently given to Buy to Let landlords?

To maintain and increase Labour's support across the young generation, the party should move to adopt this policy as one of its own. It is a perfect example of a genuinely revolutionary policy that will change the lives of young people, and it would be positioned at a time when the Conservative Party can offer only derisory reforms. The housing crisis is getting worse and is going nowhere any time soon, especially given the current government position. Corbyn must capitalise on the politicisation of this tragedy and offer the radical vision that young people are crying out for.

Richard Leonard, who succeeded Kezia Dugdale as Scottish Labour leader in November 2017, has called for rent controls north of the border, promising that if elected first minister he will introduce them. Such a move helps to demonstrate how Labour is getting it right when it comes to understanding what young people need right now.

Implementing such plans may be a different struggle altogether, but it is a necessary step in accepting that there is a real and growing crisis that demands a radical solution.

It was welcome that Corbyn announced Labour's ambition to enact rent controls in his 2017 Labour conference speech. He told the crowd in Brighton that 'rent controls exist in many cities across the world and I want our cities to have those powers too and tenants to have those protections. We also need to tax undeveloped land held by developers and have the power to compulsorily purchase.' Though some Labour councils moved to disagree with his announcement, the fact that he felt emboldened enough to make it suggests that the Labour Party will accept more radical proposals after the result of the 2017 election campaign left many surprised that so many young people were crying out for just that, a radical new settlement.

DOFF YOUR CAPS

The Intergenerational Fund found that young people's prospects had declined by more than 10 per cent between 2010 and 2015. Though now nearly three years old, this report highlighted the worsening financial crisis for them, specifically given the stagnation of wages and the rise of zero-hours contracts. For today's young people, job insecurity has become the norm. This is as much an international issue as it is a domestic one – demonstrating how crony capitalism continues to impact young people across the globe.

According to the International Labour Organization (ILO), there are 71 million unemployed young people worldwide and over 156 million young workers are living in poverty. In its biggest review of equality and inequality across the UK, the Equality and Human Rights Commission (EHRC) reported in 2015 that young people have been hit the hardest by a reduction in income and employment when compared with the older generation. The EHRC commissioner welcomed progress that had been made in some areas but highlighted the fact that though improvement had been made to level the playing field in some policy areas, young people were the ones who paid the price:

> It's great to see the barriers being lowered over the last five years for some people: but during the same period they've been raised higher for younger people in particular. Theirs are the shoulders on which the country will rely to provide for a rapidly ageing population, yet they have the worst economic prospects for several generations.

The ILO supported such an interpretation, noting that there is growing evidence in developed economies of a shift in the way poverty impacts different age groups, 'with youth taking the place of the elderly as the group at highest risk of poverty'. In a recent poll conducted by the Sutton Trust, 46 per cent of people believed that today's young people would have a worse life than their own parents' generation. Such a belief is supported by the Oxford emeritus fellow Dr John Goldthorpe, who has noted that 'a situation is emerging that is quite new in modern British history ... young people entering the labour market today face far less favourable mobility prospects than did their parents or their grandparents'. Such an announcement came shortly after Alan Milburn, then chairman of the Social Mobility and Child Poverty Commission, wrote in the *Guardian* that the UK looked set to be 'permanently divided', owing to the level of inequality between the generations.

Though some look to blame young people for the crisis in the workplace, it is not for a want of trying that they lack opportunities. Prospects – a group that aims to guide students and graduates into work or further education – found in a poll that 48 per cent of young people had undertaken an unpaid internship. What is clear, then, is that they continue to strive for better life prospects, even though inequality continues to rise between the age groups. Rather than stereotyping them as idle and lazy, it would be helpful if those in power recognised the graft of young people. It is somewhat of a cop-out that establishment commentators point to the 'changing nature of the workplace', given that artificial intelligence and automation projects have not yet eliminated the jobs that young people strive for, and they don't offer any solutions to the issue of automation anyway.

I refuse to accept that the rise of zero-hours contracts – which, according to the Office for National Statistics, disproportionally impact the young – has more to do with automation than it does the exploitation of the work force by greedy and unscrupulous bosses and boardrooms. In March 2017, it was found that the number of young people relying on zero-hours contracts in the final three months of 2016 had surged by 13 per cent compared with the same period in 2015. The total number of zero-hours contracts stood at 1.7 million, which was up from 1.4 million in 2015.

Though many argue that the contracts provide flexibility for workers, as someone who was worked under a zero-hours contract, this flexibility seems to be afforded overwhelmingly to the employer. Those in the Conservative Party who jump to the defence of the practice would do well to work under a zero-hours contract before pontificating. The public cases of exploitation should be enough to deter Conservative MPs from praising the widespread use of the contracts. Let us not forget that at Sports Direct – a company that uses the contracts very widely – an employee could hand in a sick note and on the same day be sacked without the need for an explanation.

I wrote an article for the *Independent* during the second Labour leadership election where Jeremy Corbyn's opponent, Owen Smith, disgracefully compared the leadership of the party to the managerial practice of Sports Direct. I wrote that it was important to remember some of the horrific cases that had been exposed by an investigation into the company:

Women have spoken of being forced to publicly talk about their periods in order to explain why they had been off sick. One woman even gave birth in the warehouse toilets in fear of losing her job. At that same warehouse, 110 ambulances or paramedic cars were called to deal with health and safety issues. Fifty of those cases were deemed as 'life-threatening'. Workers have spoken about being subject to strip and search procedures on their way home, often after having clocked out hours earlier than home time, working for free to keep the supervisor happy, which was necessary to keep their jobs secure.

John McDonnell's pledge during the 2017 election campaign to place policies such as banning zero-hours contracts and halting unpaid internships as 'the cornerstone of the next Labour government's programme to bring an end to the rigged economy that many experience in workplaces across Britain' was a welcome contrast to Theresa May's refusal even to discuss the impact of zero-hours contracts, given that workers apparently wanted them.

The contracts that the young are forced to work under as they enter the world of work remain exploitative and off-putting. Even those happy to work under them must ask what price is worth paying for the apparent 'flexibility' such arrangements offer. If a worker is fortunate enough to have an employer in a family business who is willing to open the shop around hours suitable to them, then I can see how this reasoning might hold. But that is not what zero-hours contracts exist for. Their widespread use is a scar on the British economy. Used by massive corporations to keep costs low, the benefits of the contracts are overwhelmingly felt by the employers and not the employees – no wonder, then, that the Conservative Party, beholden to the interests of the board-room, continues to support the extension of these contracts.

As if the structure under which young people work was not grossly unfair enough, on the issue of pay the problem only gets worse. The fact that the Tory version of the 'national living wage' – which is nearly £1 below the Living Wage Foundation recommended hourly rate – applies only to those over the age of twenty-five shows how undervalued young people are in today's society. The decision to introduce the rate for those over the age of twenty-five in April 2016 demonstrates the true extent of interest that the Conservative Party have in young people simply trying to get by.

The idea behind the introduction of the new national living wage was supposedly to allow people to have enough to 'live on'. What on earth did the Conservative government think that young people would make of this? For many, it simply made the point that the government did not believe they were worthy of a wage that they could simply scrape by on. This discrepancy on pay seems embedded in British society, with 16- and 17-year-olds also paid less than the 'Youth Development Rate' of the national minimum wage afforded to those who are eighteen to twenty. Those under twenty-five who miss out on the supposed national living wage are then placed on the rather patronising 'adult' rate of the national minimum wage, as if those aged under twenty-one are kids in the workplace.

The explanation for this inequality given by the government seems to centre on the question of experience. This is stupid. The government's position is so insulting that it does not deserve any consideration. If someone starts a job at a shop aged twenty-five with no previous retail experience, they are paid the national living wage of £7.50 (as of publication); by comparison, a 24-year-old with no retail experience will be offered £7.05 an hour, a 19-year-old with no retail experience would be paid £5.60 and a 17-year-old would be paid £4.05. None of these people has any retail experience. They are discriminated against purely because of their age.

The situation is worse for those on apprentice contracts, with those aged sixteen to eighteen paid a derisory £3.50 an hour, while those over the age of eighteen are afforded the national minimum wage relevant to their age group. Despite this, most commentary or analysis on pay at work focuses on age discrimination that affects older workers. Young people are regularly blamed for 'pushing' older people out of the workforce and the policy of age discrimination helps nobody, as it also ends up forcing discrimination against the old, who can be seen as too expensive compared to young people entering the workforce. Despite that, it is plain to see that the older you are, the more privileged position you generally have in the workplace. It is wrong to suggest that this is a crisis created by young people – it is a decision that is enforced by the government itself.

The way to tackle this disgrace is, fortunately, already Labour Party policy. When pushed on whether Labour's £10 an hour national living wage pledge would apply to 16-year-olds, Jeremy Corbyn said that the policy 'should apply to all workers'. The warning that came from the British Chambers of Commerce – that young people would be priced out of the workplace – is one business groups return to every single time workers are offered the prospect of a pay rise. It is no wonder that young people working long hours to provide for themselves, or to support themselves through sixth form and university, turned to the Labour leader in such great numbers. For as long as the Conservative Party offers division on pay where the Labour Party offers equality of earnings, there will only be one real option for them.

There also remains a racial dynamic to youth unemployment. This is an institutional problem that needs tackling. Recent data released by the Office for National Statistics suggests that black male graduates in London are almost twice as likely to be unemployed as their white counterparts. Research by the National Audit Office shows that young black men consistently have the lowest chance of gaining employment along with young Pakistani and Bangladeshi women. FullFact pointed out in 2012 that Diane Abbott – now Labour's shadow home secretary – had actually understated her claim that 44 per cent of young black people were unemployed.

Though the employment figures have changed somewhat since 2012, the difference between white and black youngsters remains similarly striking in 2017. The unemployment rate among black 16–24-year-olds was reported as being 30 per cent, which was well in excess of double the rate for white youngsters. A report released by 'Operation Black Vote' ahead of the 2017 general election noted that in '31 out of 50 of the most marginal seats in the UK, the numbers of BME electorate dwarfs the majority by which the seat was won'. This campaign made its first demand that the government should 'address black youth unemployment running at 50 per cent'.

The rise in youth turnout at the 2017 general election occurred alongside an increase in the BME vote among all age groups, which Ipsos MORI's 'How Britain Voted' survey predicted climbed by 6 per cent. They added that the Labour Party won 73 per cent of the BME vote. It is clear that youth unemployment, especially among the BME population, helped bring more young people to the ballot box after the clear focus on this issue from the Labour campaign.

Security at work is not just about being able to afford a roof over your head. Having secure, well-paid and challenging work can be a fulfilling part of normal life. What we are finding then, owing to such things being a luxury for young people today, is that normal life is no longer 'normal'. A study by the UCL Institute of Education found that 'having a zero-hours contract and being unemployed were associated with poorer self-assessed general health' and that 'those with zero-hours contracts ... were at a greater risk of reporting poor mental health after taking into account individual and behavioural characteristics'.

How can it be acceptable that our current employment system not only hits young people the hardest on job security and pay, but also impacts on their health? It is a great injustice of our time that such inequality exists in the labour market, while the government gets away with dividing our society into groups of 'strivers' and 'shirkers'. Despite their rhetoric about working hard and the value of pulling yourself up by your bootstraps, the Conservative Party continues to preside over a situation that abuses and exploits young people. Asking for more will only be the start of this surge in engagement – soon, our generation will rightly be demanding it.

Money for Nothing

On 8 October 2008, Labour Chancellor of the Exchequer Alistair Darling announced a bank rescue package totalling £500 billion. £400 billion of the scheme was 'fresh money' – that is, the Bank of England's 'Special Liquidity Scheme' already had £100 billion saved in a system for short-term loans. The plan was supported by the Conservative

Party, with then Shadow Chancellor George Osborne replying to the introduction of the plan by saying that this marked 'the final chapter of the age of irresponsibility'. With roughly £37 billion share purchase injected into Royal Bank of Scotland, Lloyds TSB and other participants, the government set into motion a plan that would see the taxpayer in control of 72 per cent of shares at RBS, 42 per cent of shares in Lloyds.

Prime Minister Gordon Brown told the public that this was 'not just money being pumped in' and that the government would sell the shares when they produced a profit. Almost a decade later, in April 2017, Tory Chancellor Philip Hammond told MPs that 'we have to live in the real world' and that this stake in RBS will likely be sold at a loss, even though the money spent on Lloyds TSB shares had more or less been recouped. The tax money we paid to bail out the banks and the money printed on our behalf by the Bank of England will never be repaid.

I make this point to highlight the fact that we have printed vast amounts of 'new' money before and it was not an issue. But what seemed to make it acceptable in that instance was that the money was printed for them, not to help us. When I say 'them', I am referring to the British establishment and, in this case, the financial establishment whose reckless greed crashed our economy and ruined lives.

The Bank of England continues to inject billions of pounds' worth of 'new' money into the UK economy. As the *Daily Telegraph* noted in 2017: 'Banks and businesses have taken full advantage of the Bank of England's quantitative easing scheme rolled out last year, borrowing far more than anticipated from the central bank.' This isn't to say that the government did the wrong thing in saving the banking sector – it is, after all, true that the collapse of the banks would have brought more misery. The point that annoys so many people is that the money always seems to be there for the rich and the powerful when they need it, but it is always too difficult or too expensive when we do.

Young people are not as fortunate as banks when it comes to investment. The money that the government places in the education budget continues to fall on a per-pupil basis. When we go to university, we are told to invest in our futures ourselves, paying £9,250 a year for such a luxury. Many of us are forced into greater levels of debt by maintenance loans owing to being from less fortunate backgrounds. When the government bailed out the banks, we were told that we were investing for the future. Why, then, do we have to keep on printing money for the City of London and its financial institutions, without any sign of a proper repayment?

Perhaps the greatest lie told by politicians is that we do not have enough money, or, as Theresa May told a hard-up nurse live on television during the general election campaign, 'There is no magic money tree.' But there is a magic money tree. There is enough money to renovate Buckingham Palace at the drop of a hat. There is enough money for May to suddenly find £1.5 billion to agree a supply-and-demand deal with the DUP. There is enough money to fund corporation tax cuts, inheritance tax cuts and a range of other benefits that improve the lives of the super wealthy. Though the government likes to suggest that tax receipts are up even though cuts in taxation rates have been made, they do so on comparing current figures to the financial years 2009-10, when the country was in the pit of a recession. As Professor Emeritus Mary Mellor of the University of Northumbria argues, there are actually two magic money trees: 'Both the state and the banks can create money out of thin air.'

The quantitative easing that we continue to see puts billions of pounds into the City of London and not into the wider economy – it mainly boosts the lives of a small elite while the rest of us pay for it. The Conservative government has successfully managed to transform the debate on economics to one that centres on the household analogy: that the government runs the country as if it was a family home. The argument suggests that the UK continues to live beyond its means, that future generations have been saddled with unsustainable debt and that difficult choices must be made, such as making cuts to public services. But this is a lie. My flat does not have its own central bank and currency. I sadly have no mechanism for creating money out of thin air. But the government does.

As Paul Mason has argued: 'Just as the peoples of Europe have a say in the tax and spend policies of their own governments they should take democratic control of monetary policy.' Mason goes further to challenge the central point of the theory: 'Quantitative easing (QE) can be designed either to benefit the rich and the financial sector, or to benefit workers, consumers, pensioners and the unemployed.'

Why is this relevant to education? Because at the centre of Jeremy Corbyn's 2015 leadership campaign was the idea of having the Bank of England create money for government investment, a plan he dubbed 'People's Quantitative Easing'.

Rival leadership candidate Yvette Cooper called the plan economically illiterate and warned that Corbyn's proposals were 'not credible or radical'. Economist Professor Richard Murphy disagreed. He had formulated the precursor to People's Quantitative Easing, 'Green Quantitative Easing', in 2010. As Murphy explains: 'In this alternative form of QE the money created by the Bank of England is provided to a National Investment Bank to inject into the real economy.' Though talk of such spending may seem somewhat distant from the energetic engagement of young people, we should make it a central part of our campaign. It is relevant because the Labour Party could, and should, use this mechanism to wipe all historic student debt.

We could call it the 'Young Plan' in homage to the Marshall Plan, but after noting this title I realised that it is also my surname, so perhaps not! The truth is that reclaiming the narrative on the economy is pretty much the key to everything, particularly when it comes to winning the wider economy. Exposing the myth of austerity being an economic necessity is key here, and it can be done by demonstrating the fact that the Conservative Party is more than happy to shake the magic money tree for their friends in the City.

The best way to respond to the constant attack that Jeremy Corbyn promised to wipe student debt would be to turn around and say: we will. What the recent outcry has shown is that there seems to be few instances where the press will engage with what the Labour Party promises. Instead, it is easier to attack the proposal or to seemingly take orders from Tory spin doctors.

As student loan debt continues to rise, the government

accepts the fact that over two-thirds of students will never pay this debt back. New analysis produced by the Institute for Fiscal Studies, produced in September 2017, demonstrated that writing off existing loans to that group of students may cost the government as little as £10 billion. Jo Johnson, the Conservative universities minister, had previously said that any plan to scrap historic student debt would cost the public in excess of £100 billion, though this assumes that every penny would be repaid instantly. Given such research from the IFS, Corbyn's promise to 'deal with' existing student debts – whatever you took that to mean – seems entirely achievable.

In its research, the IFS also stated that wiping the debt accumulated by graduates who had paid the £9,000 rate would 'have almost no effect on government debt in the short run'. Dealing with this excessive debt in such a way would be a good start for any party willing to push the reset button for young people, who continue to get the worst of all deals. If the British economy can manage with hundreds of billions of pounds being injected into financial institutions, those who argue it cannot cope with this sort of direct investment must take us for fools.

Chapter 6

Getting Involved

More Young Faces, Please

Given Jeremy Corbyn's seniority, you may be forgiven for wondering why the age of our politicians matters. Though true that Jeremy Corbyn was able to galvanise the support of the young at the fine age of sixty-eight, we would be fooling ourselves if we didn't address the lack of young voices within Parliament itself. But we have to realise that our involvement must go deeper than him alone. I believe that the best way to do this would be to install young voices within the heart of the political process, within Westminster itself. At a time when young people seem to be becoming more engaged with politics than ever before, it does not make sense for our politicians to continue without the involvement of new, young voices.

As has been discussed, one of the most damaging things about politics is that upon first interaction it is seen as the province of the old. It appears that politics exists for an older generation and that political candidates and elected officials must therefore be old too. If the first encounter young people have with politics instantly tells them that it is not for them, why should anybody be surprised that they do not wish to engage themselves with it?

There is a strange occurrence within politics whereby politicians talk about their 'vision' for the future, often without engaging the very people whose future they wish to decide. Historically, no attention has been given to the concerns of young people because they could simply be ignored without consequence. The view of most parties – including the Labour Party – was that overturning the historic pattern of low turnout among the young was a task too difficult to attempt. In this sense, it was perfectly logical to ignore the concerns of the young and also to levy the pain of austerity on their backs. If there was to be no backlash at the ballot box, then there was nothing to be worried about. It is for this reason that we have ended in the squalid situation of young people being in the most precarious position for a generation. Thankfully, this is an ill that Jeremy Corbyn reversed during the 2017 general election. It is now clear that when inspired to do so, young people will take the opportunity to voice their opinions at the ballot box.

But what if young people had something more than a national campaign taking place every five years to back? What if they could go to the ballot box on election day knowing that they could elect a representative who had their firm interest at heart? Encouraging young people to stand for office is an important step in reconnecting with them, insofar as it offers the belief that they could have a representative not too dissimilar from themselves. This is particularly important at a time when the Conservative Party appears to grow ever older.

The Labour Party could capitalise on this opportunity by making their own party look younger. The most recent example of such a move comes from the Scottish National Party. At just twenty years old, Mhairi Black made history in 2015 after defeating Shadow Foreign Secretary Douglas Alexander to his Paisley and Renfrewshire South seat – a constituency that had been Labour for seventy years. Black has proved to be one of the most competent and engaging parliamentarians in recent history, despite those that attempt to denigrate her for her age.

At this last election, Black called on young people to vote in greater numbers than they had ever before: 'The Tories think they can do anything they want to young people and get away with it – from hiking tuition fees to slashing housing benefit for young people and much more. That's why it is so important that young people turn up and vote – don't let the Tory government leave you behind.'

Black's words were made more powerful by virtue of her being young and directly connected to the concerns of her generation. Black also seems supportive of the fact that Corbyn's 'listening exercise' was more powerful than any attempt to be seen as 'down with the kids' through the cheap gimmicks we have been used to. Black has previously said that she was 'sick of folk mentioning' her age in the press and in the House, reporting that 'during the campaign, no one asked about my age, it was all in-depth political questions'. Furthermore, she said that 'trying to tailor politics to be "young, hip and cool" is exactly the kind of patronising guff that puts off young folk. If you want to talk to young folk about politics then just talk politics. They will listen.'

This certainly seems to be the case, given that this recent election campaign saw few gimmicks and more genuine substance when it came to appealing to the young. The old and embarrassing examples of engaging with the young, such as Blair's dad-dancing around the time of the 'Cool Britannia' wave, have been swept aside and replaced by a genuinely modern and comfortable approach. Young people are finally being approached on their own terms and spoken to about real issues – that is what got them so engaged in the first place and it must now continue to be the case.

This is not to say that young people necessarily wish to represent their own age group alone. But those opposed to young candidates do not have a solid argument to make. Given that Parliament has always been tipped in favour of the old, it is about time that its hallways and chambers were filled with innovative young voices. Politics must move beyond answering the question of why politicians need to make themselves more relatable to the young by asking why there are so few young elected representatives, and what can they do to ensure more of them are elected.

In Corbyn, young people found something of a role model, a politician to aspire to. His legacy could very well be the fact that young people feel inspired to enter the political arena in a similar authentic and honourable spirit, rather than doing so for the gravy train. At a time when they felt that they had lost any sense of value, Corbyn's inspiring message provided an outlet for expressing this.

The 2017 Young People's Wellbeing Report demonstrates

how deep this sense really was. The proportion of young people showing signs of depression or anxiety rose sharply after the 2008 financial crash and has not got any better since. The proportion of young people living in households with less than 60 per cent of the median income continues to rocket. When asked if they feel that they belonged to their neighbourhood, they split roughly 50/50 in agreeing whether they did or not. Without young champions in their own neighbourhoods to invest in, it is unsurprising that they turned to the national political arena. And the scale of that problem is clear when you realise that the average age of a local councillor in 2013 was 60.2 years, according to the Census of Local Authority Councillors, and 60.8 per cent of local councillors were over the age of sixty. It is hardly an inspiring picture.

Encouraging young people to stand for elected office would be one way of attacking this status quo head-on. Though inexperience is often used as an excuse to bar them from political office, I believe that this is a trait that should be seen as a useful one. In some ways, our freshness should be seen as a blessing rather than a curse. We are not indebted to any organisation or business that has placed us at the centre of the political process. We owe nothing to nobody. Our political engagement has come about by the belief that we could actually change things – not because it was promoted by some shadowy group.

With any luck, a desire to stand will simply be a natural extension of the increased engagement we witnessed at this recent general election. But it is not good enough for us to sit on our hands and hope for the best anymore. This is perhaps the most pertinent point of this recent general election: we have demonstrated that action works, that being involved in the political process can change things. Importantly, we have given Corbyn an endorsement that allows the left to tell the disaffected that not all politicians are the same. Those of us who have offered this endorsement now have a duty to encourage and support more of our own generation to become active and involved.

But how do we encourage those who are still not sure of politics to become involved, never mind stand for office? One of the simple changes we can make is to ensure that politics is social, which means getting people out and campaigning together. Ahead of the Oldham West and Royton by-election in 2015, Labour's surging membership was criticised for its apparent failure to turn out and campaign. I said at the time that one of the greatest problems with socialism was that it always required explanation.

When I am out campaigning, I speak to people who often seem to be instinctively supportive of socialism and who see it as a rational option after a few minutes of conversation. But when you are on the doorstep, talking to voters about Labour's offer, those minutes certainly add up. In that by-election, UKIP had the advantage of shouting about immigration while having to offer very little in terms of substance. Their simple message was easily understood, which gave them an advantage.

But the Labour Party under Corbyn has gained a great weapon when it comes to youth engagement: a mass of devoted, passionate members who are more than willing to have these conversations. With more and more people joining, the party was able to have serious discussions with more of the electorate. During the 2017 general election, I helped to campaign in the marginal seat of Lincoln and I organised a youth campaigning day where dozens of young people took part in very serious and meaningful debates with many who were sometimes four times their age. The new politics has got to be about engaging with people in a serious, focused and nuanced way, rather than simply asking how they will vote. And there is no better demographic to spark these conversations than the young and the curious.

Understandably, many might feel nervous about engaging in political conversations with those they don't know, by knocking on the doors of strangers. Having such discussions with friends is an easy way to start the process, and it can even help engage more young people. Just being brave enough to say that you are interested and that you care about politics will often be enough to spark some form of conversation. As many of us know, it may sometimes lead to a heated and negative debate that concentrates on the idea that politics doesn't change anything and that all politicians are the same, but at least you can move on from that point.

We are fortunate that the 2017 election has reinvigorated a strong interest in politics among the young. But making it last is what is most important. Some are certain that this fact alone is all that matters. James Kenney, an 18-year-old student, told me: 'Now that young people know they have the power to radically change the country through the power of the vote, more people will do it.' Similarly, Rhys Warner, twenty-one, explained to me that politics isn't something 'that's turned on and off'.

I am inclined to believe this and I am confident that those

who were involved in this election will remain engaged. But what concerns me is ensuring that the next generation, the next change-makers, are offered a similar chance to get involved. Though it remains a mystery as to when the next election will be called, if it is 2022 as scheduled, some of us who were 'young' for this last contest could be nearly thirty by the next. In fact, people as young as thirteen then may have the vote at the next election. This is why we need deep and lasting structural change and it is why the Conservative government remains so opposed to real citizenship education in schools.

My political education was an extracurricular one – politics was never discussed formally throughout my education until I could study it in sixth form. It is somewhat of an anomaly that we are taught the history of our democracy and our political system while never being given the opportunity to engage with it. The national curriculum omits politics in its entirety, even if some schools occasionally find time for it. This is what worries me when it comes to future engagement. Young people shouldn't have to chance upon politics if a politician such as Jeremy Corbyn happens to come along – it should be a fact that is embedded within normal life. We will find it hard to have young candidates for political office if we do not ensure that this election was not just a one-night stand; we want young people to become lifelong political activists, after all.

We already know that little evidence exists to suggest that young people are more apathetic than older generations. So why is it that so few people under the age of thirty stand for political office if these structural issues do not matter? There are a number of measures that we must look at in order to both boost engagement further and make our Parliament younger and more representative. Some measures are more controversial than others but it is important to assess them in sum. Though real change will require radical institutional reform, such as lowering the voting age or introducing compulsory voter registration, there are cultural and social steps that we can all take to encourage political activism among the young, from changing the attitudes of the old, through direct conversations with our own parents and grandparents to forming groups that promote political literacy. The issue of disengagement goes beyond the realm of politics alone. For too long, young people have been made to feel as if they are a nuisance, despite their own best efforts to become active citizens. We need a radical settlement within our political system if we are to improve on current levels of engagement, advance from this new baseline and get young voices into the heart of Westminster.

One product of the 2017 general election has been the welcome addition to the House of Commons of Laura Pidcock, the new MP for North West Durham. Pidcock was elected at just twenty-nine years old and has already proved to be one the Labour Party's most effective modern politicians in a matter of months. Her maiden speech, in which she stated that Parliament 'reeks of the establishment, and of power' with its confusing systems built at a time when 'my class and my sex would have been denied a place in it because we were deemed unworthy', went viral online and sent alarm bells ringing in the Conservative Party.

She later caused controversy when she was interviewed

about being friends with her Tory colleagues after stating: 'Whatever type they are, I have absolutely no intention of being friends with any of them.' What Pidcock was alluding to was the fact that she had no interest in joining members on the Strangers Terrace for glasses of champagne after they had just voted through legislation that would harm her constituents. Pidcock's comments were decried by a political class used to the chumminess of the New Labour era as 'hateful'. Such commentators missed the point entirely. What she represents is a new generation of Labour politicians unwilling to trade their class and convictions in the members' lobby for a seat on the green benches.

The young, northern and working-class grit with which Pidcock has already challenged the Westminster establishment is exactly what the Labour Party and our tired institutions need so desperately. With a handful of other young MPs elected at the 2017 general election, one can only hope that such attitudes will serve to change the Labour Party for the better as it moves forward. Though no one need discuss a successor for Jeremy Corbyn at this point in time, picking one from this new generation would show the sincerity of Labour's respect for hard-working and capable young people.

Seeing more young faces at the heart of our democracy must be the aim of our movement. We must not understate how powerful this would be in ensuring that future generations know that politics exists for them, too. The question, then, is how we get there and how we ensure that the legacy of the 2017 general election is about so much more than the political gossip surrounding Theresa May and the dumbfounding of columnists convinced that Corbyn would fail. Instead, we can forge the way to ensure that it marks the birth of a new political era, where young people stand ready to claim their place in society and to demand radical change that will ensure our voices are never banished from the political system ever again.

A Democratic Scandal

In 2010, at the age of fourteen, I was elected to the UK Youth Parliament, an elected body of young politicians voted for by young people across constituencies, with the sole intention of campaigning vigorously for the reduction in the voting age to sixteen. Shortly after my election, I penned a letter to David Cameron calling on him to support a reduction in the voting age. Ahead of the 2010 leadership election, I received personal support for the campaign from both Ed and David Miliband as they vied for the top position.

In the letter that I sent to the prime minister, I asked how it could possibly be fair to exclude 16- and 17-year-olds from the ballot given that they are able to contribute to the taxes that pay their MP, join the armed forces with a view to fight for their MP and, if they were so inclined, legally marry and have sex with their MP. I only ever received a confirmation receipt from the prime minister's office in reply to my letter. Now, some eight years later, I remain as steadfast in my support for the reduction of the voting age as I was when I was fourteen years old. It is perhaps the single most important thing that we must argue for in terms of creating a lasting coalition of young voters, and I was proud to see Jeremy Corbyn's manifesto back the call to correct this outdated policy of disenfranchisement.

My personal belief in lowering the voting age has always relied on what I see as the convincing 'Why not?' argument as quoted above. If we entrust 16- and 17-year-olds with great responsibilities in other areas of their lives, how is it fair to deny them a basic civic responsibility? An anonymous contribution to YouGov's panel on the lowering of the voting age debate made this point rather succinctly:

> At sixteen years of age you are able to marry, pay taxes and leave home. You can legally have sex, which implies it is the age at which the government deems you old enough to become a parent. If you are deemed old enough to become a parent, get married and contribute to the Treasury, then you should be deemed old enough to decide who makes the policies that so greatly affect your life.

Quite. It remains a shocking fact that young people are denied the right to choose the government that could quite happily arm them in order to defend the nation. The backwardness of this premise remains a confusing one. I find it difficult to understand opposition to this point – how can debates be had concerning the point at which a child becomes an adult when opponents to votes at sixteen entrust young people with the institution of marriage and tax? The major inconsistencies on when one becomes an 'adult' have simply been accepted rather than dealt with. It is more than unfortunate that this debate has been allowed to run on for decades. In fact, it is unjust.

It does not make sense to afford young people with adult responsibilities while simultaneously denying them the full stretch of adult rights. There is a misplaced view that young people below the age of eighteen are not contributing members of our society. My own experience proves that this is not the case. When I was sixteen years old and doing my A-Levels, I worked part-time at the weekend in order to ensure that I could pay for books. Given the chronic underfunding of the education system, my school could not afford anything that was up to date and so it fell on students to be able to keep informed.

Earning £3.50 an hour didn't get you very far, though. Most days I would spend half of my earnings on the bus to and from work and my lunch. Every day I contributed to my local economy, whether it be the bus company or the place that I would buy food. I was also working – both employed and in full-time education. I was doing exactly what is asked of all of us, but I received no real reward for it. This is the same story for many people my age. It is why so many decided that it was time to get involved at this election, because for so long we had been sold a vision that never seemed to come to fruition.

Being politically active and having campaigned for the voting age to be lowered, I was all too aware of the fact that I was also denied the right to vote in any election. And for some people I was working with, who were in the same year at school but some eight months younger, their right to vote in a general election would not even come into force until this recent general election. That's nearly five years of working before being given the right to vote on national issues that directly impact young people, their futures and their jobs.

And it isn't just in employment that young people are given adult responsibilities. The growing care crisis in Britain means that more and more young people are being relied on as primary caregivers for members of their family. Census figures suggest that there are at least 376,000 young adult carers in the UK who are permitted to give what is often round-the-clock care to their relatives. I raise this point not just because of the monumental and heroic job that these young people are tasked to do, but because under the rollout of Universal Credit the Severe Disability Premium is cut, with the Children's Society estimating that families with a young carer will be £2,876 a year worse off because of this cut. Given that these young people are not afforded the vote, they have absolutely no way of contesting this cut or making their voices heard.

To make matters worse, the Enhanced Disability Premium also looks set to be abolished, meaning that families with a young carer looking after a disabled relative will lose more than £3,500 a year. How can this be just? How can the government levy such pain and austerity on young people making a heroic sacrifice while at the same time denying them the right to have their say on this issue? Young people have been given more adult responsibilities while being refused the most basic adult responsibility of all. We expect them to deal with so much more than we once did, and yet we deny them any form of power over the decisions made in Westminster which serve to directly impact their lives.

It is not just a question of unfairness. There are serious and convincing arguments regarding what lowering the voting age can achieve in terms of engagement that also serve as solid reasoning to back the move. Evidence continues to point to the fact that voting is a habitual act, so when someone votes in an election it makes them more likely to vote in the next. Lowering the voting age would allow for an establishment of new and young voters who would be more likely to continue voting for the rest of their lives.

Much of the reasoning behind this rests with the argument of socialisation. Young people at the age of sixteen remain in constant contact with friends and colleagues at school and work. Those under the age of eighteen are still likely to be living at home and remain connected to the community in which they live and serve, which means voting would more than likely be a topic of discussion come election time. This recent election demonstrates that if young people are made to feel involved and valued, they will remain interested and in turn will be more likely to vote.

Given the recent rise in turnout, opening our democracy to more young people is a sure way to continue the fight against the democratic deficit in the UK. The historic decision to allow 16- and 17-year-olds the right to vote in the Scottish independence referendum serves as an example of this. In March 2014, the Scottish government estimated that over 80 per cent of this age group had registered to vote. At the time, the number of 18–25-year-olds registered to vote across the UK was just 55 per cent. An ICM survey conducted after the referendum found that 75 per cent of 16- and 17-year-olds voted in that referendum. Though still somewhat less than the figure for the older generations, this was a staggering victory for those who argue – like myself – that young people wish to be involved in politics. The enthusiasm with which young Scots participated in the ballot is proof that our voting age should be lowered across the UK. What young people in Scotland proved was that there is no such thing as political apathy among the young – we are just waiting to be engaged and given the permission to take part.

And though 16- and 17-year-olds were not able to vote in the 2017 election, it didn't stop them from becoming engaged. Many that I have spoken to noted their frustration at not being able to vote, but said that they were pleased they were able to get involved in the campaign through traditional and online activism. The fact that they are registering their frustration with the enforced detachment from the electoral system is a sign that it is time our politicians did something to involve 16- and 17-year-olds in the political process.

Take student James Barber, who told me: 'I'm only seventeen, so I couldn't vote. But as the youth officer for my constituency, it was my responsibility to get young people to vote.' Charlotte Cochrane also explained that this exclusion was something that continued to put people off: 'The young are treated with such disdain because the older generation refuse to believe that we are capable of making such large decisions, especially when it comes to picking our own prime minister . . . young people are always treated like their opinions do not matter and that delicate and important discussions should be left to the older generation.' It seems that denying interested and passionate young people the right to vote simply confirms their worst suspicions about an out-of-touch system that does nothing for them.

The argument that political education is necessary before the lowering of the voting age is also a tired one. Ideally, I would agree that the introduction of a genuine political curriculum would be beneficial before extending the franchise. But we are not in an ideal world. We are in a world where even this compromise has been scoffed at for decades, without ever getting any closer to achieving both aims. What I propose is that any party wanting to engage young people should actually push for the enfranchisement of 16- and 17-year-olds as a way to force political education onto the agenda.

It is, after all, the case that we do not ask eighteen-year-olds – or sixty-year-olds for that matter – to take part in years of political education before we offer them the vote. It's time for organisations such as the UK Youth Parliament and the British Youth Council to become much more radical in their campaigning. Young people are being denied the vote and this is now an explicitly political issue, with the Labour Party promising to introduce votes at sixteen and the Tories refusing even to consider the proposal. For youth bodies to ignore the inherently party-political nature of this debate does a disservice to those they claim to represent. Though great that the UK Youth Parliament manages to hold a national annual debate with its members in the House of Commons, its aim should be to have some of those same young people in the House on a full-time basis. To achieve that, it needs to get on board with the political debate. Even if that means politicising the Youth Parliament, it should happen – have candidates run on a partisan basis rather than as local youth representatives and see how quickly the organisation would become an effective campaigning body.

Given that this has become a political issue, it is important to ask the question why the Tories still remain opposed to the plan to reduce the voting age. Could it be that they believe 16- and 17-year-olds are not mature enough to vote? No. The simple answer is that they know they would likely never win power again. Using the latest Office for National Statistics population data per parliamentary constituency, it is possible to estimate how many 16- and 17-year-olds there are in each given parliamentary seat. We can then apply a 72 per cent turnout rate of this age group, the upper estimate of youth turnout in the 2017 general election, to predict the impact. Though no specific polling of this age range was conducted prior to the general election, using the 18–24 polling by ICM for Hope Not Hate prior to the election day, which estimated 68 per cent would vote Labour and 16 per cent for the Conservatives, it is possible to predict which seats would have changed hands.

Of the ten most marginal Conservative/Labour seats (Southampton Itchen, Preseli Pembrokeshire, Pudsey, Thurrock, Hastings & Rye, Chipping Barnet, Norwich North, Calder Valley, Aberconwy and Stoke-On-Trent South), nine would have changed hands and moved into Labour control. Aberconwy would be the only seat on this list that would remain Conservative, albeit by 120 votes. We all know the impact that this would have had on the outcome of the election. Theresa May would not have had enough seats to form a supply-and-demand deal with the DUP and it is likely that another election would have had to have been called, given the united opposition the Tories would have faced on issues such as the Great Repeal Bill from the Labour Party, the SNP and the Liberal Democrats. Even a lesser turnout of 62 per cent of 16- and 17-year-olds would have seen these seats change hands, most likely ensuring May's resignation and another election, which the Tories would have entered battered and bruised by a surging Jeremy Corbyn.

This is, of course, purely hypothetical. The only statistical certainty is that these seats would have been Labour as per the data provided. Though we cannot be sure whether May would have resigned or attempted to stumble on with a minority government, the frailty of the Conservative government today, even with its deal with the DUP, suggests that the prime minister would have had little room for manoeuvre. The magnitude of such a change should not be understated. Had 16- and 17-year-olds been able to vote in the 2017 general election, we can assume that things would look very different: there would have been no bitter deal with the DUP, May would likely be out of Downing Street, the Tories would be gripped in disarray between Brexit and a looming leadership contest, and Corbyn would be in an even stronger position than the one that he holds today – all with another general election on the horizon. It is quite obvious, then, why the Conservative Party should be so opposed to lowering the voting age. For the dying breed to legislate for more of its opponents to gain the right to vote would really be a case of the turkeys voting for Christmas.

Given the recent surge in support for the Labour Party, things only look worse for the Conservative Party should these 16- and 17-year-old votes be added into a predictor for the next election. Many polls point towards Labour gaining ground as the Conservatives slip back. On a uniform national swing, where the gap between the two parties was around

5 per cent, the Labour Party would gain sixty-one seats and the Conservative Party would lose fifty-five, placing the Labour Party some three seats short of an overall majority. Such a poll would bring another set of Conservative seats into the extreme marginal category, where any seat with less than an 800-vote majority would be likely to swing to Labour on the basis of 16- and 17-year-olds being allowed the vote. In short, with these votes, Labour would not just remove the Conservatives from power, it would gain an overall majority without the need for a coalition or a supply-and-demand deal.

Given that such a result would see the Tories lose the likes of Justine Greening, Amber Rudd, Stephen Crabb, Iain Duncan Smith and Nicky Morgan, it is unlikely that we will see the Conservative Party shift its support behind the campaign to lower the voting age. A 5 per cent swing from the Conservative Party to the Labour Party with the top-up of 16- and 17-year-old votes could see Conservative seats with as much as a 5,000 vote majority put at risk – including seats such as Uxbridge and South Ruslip, the constituency of Foreign Secretary Boris Johnson. So while it is unlikely the Conservative Party will even consider lowering the voting age in their pitch to young people, it is important to remember how important such a move could be in transforming the political map of the country. It also shows why it is vital that Labour makes the argument for this change central to their offer, given that it would allow them to make a real difference in the country, so long as they continue to appeal to the young people who would be happy to lend their vote to a party with their best interests at heart.

With rumours circulating at the time of writing that the Conservative Party looks set to offer young people a new deal over the next few years, this will not be accepted by young people who are well aware of the fact that their government does not believe they have the right to be heard. They will feel this way given both the fact that the Conservatives refuse to engage in the debate concerning lowering the voting age and owing to their attempts at rigging the electoral register in the year after their 2015 general election success.

The Electoral Commission noted in February 2016 that roughly 770,000 names previously registered under the household registration system had not re-registered themselves under the new system. Though introduced by Gordon Brown's Labour government, the way the plan was rolled out by the coalition government saw voters removed from the register altogether. The old system (whereby anyone could register everyone living in their households) was replaced by an individual voter registration system requiring every individual voter to sign up personally. As Labour leader in January 2015, Ed Miliband called the plan the 'final insult' Nick Clegg delivered to young people. The switch from household registration, as well as universities and colleges being banned from 'block-registering' students, was blamed as the reason for a million names dropping off the register. Though many have now signed up, they shouldn't have to do so at all.

What the Labour Party should advocate is automatic registration. Given automatic enrolment into the National Insurance system, this would not be too hard to achieve. The least registered groups are the young and those from marginalised backgrounds. The current individual registration approach does not fit with the times nor with the great democracy our country purports to be. There is no reason why existing data that the government holds on its citizens cannot be cross-referenced to automatically register voters.

Though some argue that automatic registration goes against the idea of civic duty, given that it is not compulsory to vote, this argument seems somewhat weak. The 'Electoral Management in Britain' research conducted by Dr Toby James in 2014 found that most people believe they are already registered because they pay council tax. This in turn leads to many people being turned away from polling stations on voting day. Indeed, research from Dr Alistair Clark and Dr Toby James in 2015 found that two-thirds of polling stations turned away potential voters who thought they were registered but were not. A number of European states already practise automatic enrolment and a number of states within the US do the same, offering an opt-out function. Oregon and California are among such states, registering all voters who receive a driving licence. With some engagement between departments, there is no reason that the UK government could not receive confirmation of voter registration alongside receiving their National Insurance number.

Given that nobody has to register to pay tax, it seems pertinent to ask the question as to why somebody should be forced to register for the right to vote. In making this small change, politicians could offer greater legitimacy to the current system while also engaging with all young people. Whether enrolling millions of young people on the register would be a popular Tory policy is a pertinent question, but it is also irrelevant. The question as to whether it should be Labour policy is much more important. If Labour truly wishes to represent the voices of the unheard young, then it must pledge to enrol them automatically. We can no longer exist within a system that denies 16- and 17-year-olds the vote while simultaneously erecting barriers for their political participation even when they turn eighteen.

THE TERRIFIED PARTY

Young Labour now has over 110,000 members. This makes it the third largest party in the United Kingdom, just some 7,000 behind the entire membership of the Scottish National Party and nearly double the membership of the Liberal Democrats, as per their last officially reported accounts. In comparison, Conservative MP Andrew Bowie announced in January 2018 that the Conservative Party had fewer than 10,000 members aged under thirty. It is reported from within the Labour Party, including by leading members of its youth movement and senior members of party staff, that Young Labour trebled its membership long before Corbyn success-fully trebled the membership of the whole Labour Party since his election as leader in 2015.

With young people engaging with the political system at such great levels, it is important that the very institution that should encourage such engagement is analysed. The Labour Party, its machinery and its current structures are entirely unfit for the modern day. It is no wonder that stories of young people being turned away from constituency Labour Party meetings have become so widespread. Some in the Labour Party have a tendency to weaponise political language in a way that makes its structures uncompromising and alienating. The jargon that surrounds internal Labour discussions locks the inexperienced out of the process. It is my opinion that this is often done with some malice, with older and more experienced hands wanting to preserve their grip on control within local parties. Many young people have spoken to me about being pushed into corners at party meetings; some have even been told to keep their opinions to themselves by older and more established members. Having the nerve to turn up to a meeting can be a big deal for some people and being greeted by a braying mob of supposed 'comrades' helps nothing, especially when they seem fixated on discussing a host of abbreviations that mean nothing to anybody new to it all.

Prior to Corbyn's second leadership victory there was an obvious hostility towards new members – of any age – within the Labour Party. I have heard so many stories about older cliques criticising members trying to get involved. One councillor in Manchester told me that they had attended monthly meetings where new members were denounced as 'useless muppets', with the majority feeling being that all these newcomers had signed up only to vote for Jeremy Corbyn. *Vice* reported that a former Labour prospective parliamentary candidate spoke of receiving 'abusive emails' when he contacted new members about local events, often receiving replies such as: 'I just joined to vote for Jeremy Corbyn, stop fucking emailing me.'

The belief at the time was that these members were simply voting fodder who turned up to cast a vote in the leadership election and wanted nothing more to do with the party. To me, this seemed a stupid way to deal with what was obviously a problem within the party. Rejecting new, young and enthusiastic members was unlikely to generate any better feeling. But the attitude of the established Labour Party was to continue along this line. Some in the media became fixated on the idea that Corbyn was adding members but failing to engage them and that their failure to turn out at Labour events and campaigning sessions demonstrated that the cult of personality was very real.

What the Labour Party should have done was ask the very simple question why these new members were showing up once and disappearing? Then, rather than going on some form of victim-blaming campaign, they should have looked in on themselves. What can we do to engage these newcomers? How can we make them feel welcome? Sadly, some did not want them to become engaged at all, owing to factional disputes. Why would those opposed to Corbyn want to welcome dozens – and in some places hundreds – of new, energetic, young pro-Corbyn members? The idea of them getting involved and active within local parties continues to scare those who feel bereaved after Labour's successful 2017 campaign.

But now that the power of the membership has been demonstrated, we must ask what the party can do to engage young people within their communities. The first thing that local parties should do is establish an outreach officer who can get in touch with young members directly to ensure that they are being invited to party events. Using new technology to contact these people on a personal basis will also be key to holding out an olive branch to those who had previously been kicked to the sidelines.

Party officers and elected officials should also be doing all that they can to attend youth events and to support Young Labour campaigns within their local areas. The best way to ensure that this happens is to continue reminding your local representative that their position probably relies on ensuring that this youth surge continues. Across university towns up and down the country, MPs must be reminded of the power of the youth vote. When local Labour councillors ask why young people are not turning out to campaign for them in the same way that they did for Jeremy Corbyn, they should take a long, hard look at themselves before pointing the finger at an 'inactive' membership base. There is a reason young people are willing to campaign for Corbyn and not for Labour councillors that have continued to support austerity. The reason is nothing to do with the laziness or idleness of the young and everything to do with the failure of established officials to engage with such voices.

Young people should feel comfortable in taking their rightful place at local Labour Party events and meetings. But we must also look at reforming the way that the meetings work. It's all well and good explaining how people can get involved, but that doesn't solve the fact that the meetings are often – and unnecessarily – boring and dogmatic. The 'party democracy review' that will look at ways to democratise the Labour Party is a good start when it comes to assessing how we can modernise democracy within the party. But it is important that we analyse the failings of our very fundamental structures.

The new socialism cannot rely on the old methods and the old ways of doing things – people do not feel that passing endless motions at party meetings is in any way useful. It is, of course, a basic function of what the party should be doing. But such bureaucracy needs to be accompanied by radical campaign days and outreach sessions. Some constituencies are doing this already and some are doing a good job at engaging with new members and also the wider public in light of Labour's 2017 general election result. For example, in Kensington, the CLP chair David Kear has opened the local party to campaigners and community champions in a way that has brought an entire borough together, irrelevant of their previous commitment to the party. I went to one event in London where they attempted to bridge the divide between Labour's warring factions by having a 'speed debating' session between those from different wings of the party. These are positive examples of a changing party, but such movement is not widespread. The party should be assessing how it can reform its own structure so as to make it more engaging.

Giving young people more power within the party will hopefully encourage them to get involved. It is a crying shame that the structures continue to stifle young people's engagement at a time when we should be welcoming those who helped produce such a stunning election result with open arms. Those who continue to actively discourage new young members from getting involved should face some sort of disciplinary action based on the current Labour Party rulebook for forcing people out of the party. Tactics that are utilised by some members to discourage such engagement should be recognised and called out by those who care about the future of our party. It is one thing to ensure that young people remain engaged with Labour's message at election time, but it is just as important to ensure that our own house is in order and capable of engaging with young people in the space between elections. If we fail to keep the momentum with the young and in the meantime actively push them away, we cannot turn around at the next election and stomp our feet and ask: 'Where were they this time?'

Chapter 7

Next Steps

You Ain't Seen Nothing Yet

What we know, then, is that more young people voted in this recent general election than have before. The collapse of youth turnout since 1979 has been reversed. Those voices that were long criticised for their apparent laziness made a point of turning up to the ballot box and casting what has been rightly afforded to them through the franchise. We know that in constituencies across the country this decision had a huge impact on turnout, especially in areas densely populated by young voters.

Research published by Novara Media from Mark McDonagh and Claire Frank ahead of the general election demonstrated how young voters could defeat the Tories in key marginals. One of the scenarios assessed was what would happen if half of 2015's UKIP vote switched to the Conservatives while the young voter turnout increased to the national average of 66 per cent. The model predicted that in that case twenty-four of Labour's twenty-nine most marginal seats would be saved. In fact, Labour went on to secure twenty-three of these seats, just one below the prediction published in this research.

What we also know is that young people shifted towards the left on an unprecedented scale. The support that the young now have for Jeremy Corbyn and the Labour Party appears unbreakable. At the beginning of the Conservative Party conference in 2017, nearly four months after the election was held, a survey for the Social Market Foundation by Opinium showed just how consolidated this backing has become. Among 18–24-year-olds, just 15 per cent of voters said that the Tories represent 'people like me'. Only 20 per cent of 25–34-year-olds felt the same way, and that figure reached only 21 per cent of 35–44-year-olds. Meanwhile, 76 per cent of people across all these age groups believe that the Tories serve to represent 'richer people' in politics. The Conservatives are seen as more connected to the needs of people aged over sixty-five when compared with Labour. All age groups below this top bracket believed that the Labour Party was on their side by varying majorities.

As James Kirkup, the director of the Social Market Foundation, noted: 'The Conservatives' problem is that you can't expect people to support an economic settlement in which they have literally no stake.' Andrew Cooper, former pollster to David Cameron, told the *Guardian* that the figures were an 'existential threat' to the Conservative Party. The fact that young people are embracing socialism is beyond doubt. Two conclusions can therefore be concretely confirmed: more young people are voting and, when they do, they are far more likely to vote for the Labour Party in its current form.

We know that some of the criticisms levied against Jeremy Corbyn since his election as Labour leader in September 2015 and up until the general election no longer hold. We were told that he was a weak and ineffectual leader who would not win over the country, that his popularity within the Labour Party could not be replicated in a general election. These views must now be disregarded by anybody that wishes to be taken seriously as we move forward towards the next general election. As young voices throughout this book have noted, Corbyn's leadership style is what attracts so many people. His willingness to listen openly and honestly while refusing to dictate every detail reflects a breath of fresh air in a political world that often seems micro-managed and robotic. Letting Jeremy be Jeremy proved an effective strategy during the election campaign.

Since the election, he has only served to prove his strength. Whether it be his summer of campaigning in key marginals across the country or his perfectly delivered speech at the Labour Party conference in 2017, it is obvious that he is a prime minister in waiting and not the hapless backbencher that many allowed themselves to believe he was. Confident, assured and comfortable, he has cast aside the doubts on his leadership and his position within the Labour Party is now secure. As the months go by, it will be important for him to ensure that his popularity within the country at large remains the same. Long gone are the days when David Cameron stood at the dispatch box in the House of Commons chamber and mocked the Labour leader's choice of suit. Now the Conservative Party clings to power only in the fear that Labour will romp home should another election be called.

We know that Theresa May now regrets her decision to call the snap election. Believing that she would be returned with a majority well in excess of Tony Blair's 1997 landslide, the Tories were hungry for the vote. But now they are terrified. Telling Andrew Marr that she does not regret calling the election is proof of how stale their politics has become. Do they think we are stupid? The prime minister called an election and lost her majority. Who would not regret that? Instead of being honest with the British people, the Conservative Party still trade in their PR version of politics. This is great news for a Labour Party that continues to reconnect with normal people across the country. Tired of the old politics, the young scrambled to get involved with a new politics at this last general election. Yet the Conservative Party has learned all the wrong lessons. If they think freezing tuition fees at £9,250 until 2019 is the answer, then they have surely lost it altogether. If there is a genuine belief among the Tories that tinkering at the edges will reverse their fortunes, I look forward to seeing the result of such a disastrous strategy.

What we know is that young people did not vote for free university tuition alone. They did not vote simply because they believed that the Labour Party would return their Education Maintenance Allowance. They were not bribed. Young people voted because they were sold a vision of a society that they want to take part and grow up in. They rallied behind a narrative that reflected their own desires and aspirations. The idea that the young voted for self-interested reasons must be rubbished for the falsehood that it is. In many ways, we all vote for what we believe is best anyway, but as more research emerges into this general election result, I am sure that this will be found to be the case. It is what hundreds of young people have told me every single time that I have asked the question, indeed many of them have been exasperated even to hear it muttered. It is simply a continuation of the condescending old politics that turned young people away for so long.

Though welcome that the Labour Party is now refusing to play any part in promoting that politics, it would be healthier for our democracy if all political leaders did the same. What would be best for young people would be to have a real choice between two competing visions for their futures, rather than continued disdain from a Conservative Party that has been left in panic after the young robbed them of their government majority. At this moment in time, it seems that the Labour Party is more than aware of its need to continue taking young people seriously. The early signs of the Conservative strategy suggest the opposite.

We also know that young people are terrified of what they see happening to the National Health Service, particularly mental health services. Having viewed this as the most important issue at the 2017 general election, young people have made it clear that the lack of support they are receiving through mental healthcare provision is simply unacceptable. With more young people facing episodes of depression and anxiety, a failure by any political party to tackle this tragic phenomenon will only serve to embed negative feeling across the young. There is a clear desire for a government that will attempt to make their lives somewhat more hopeful. The stresses of daily life impact us all, but with my generation set to do worse than the last, it is clear that we are facing new worries at a younger age. Until we receive the support we need to address these worries, it is likely that the mental health crisis will only deepen in this country. Making further cuts to the NHS, or failing to respect those working in the service, will damage any potential link between young people and the Conservative Party.

Young people also remain deeply concerned about their inability to live in decent rented accommodation – let alone buy their own home. The housing crisis continues to develop as the government fails to grasp the fact that we simply cannot afford to take a step onto the housing ladder no matter how generous the schemes they produce are. Removing stamp duty for first-time buyers doesn't help if you can't afford the deposit or get a mortgage in the first place. The complete failure of the prime minister to understand that the vision she sells simply does not resonate with the lives we lead will continue to haunt her party. With every announcement on housing, the Tories seem more out of touch than before. Unfortunately for May, her usual political strategy of 'polishing a turd' will not stick any longer. Young people are hungry for real change and though Labour is offering that, the Conservative Party continues to cook up half-baked policies.

On Brexit, we can accept that we know some things and not others. We know that a rather large majority of young people voted to Remain. We know that far fewer of them decided to turn out in that referendum than they did at the

2017 general election. The extent to which the issue will impact on the way they will vote next time remains unclear. I have speculated that they opted with the progressive choice during the referendum, after being turned off by a regressive and vile Leave campaign that played on fear. The entire basis of the Leave campaign went against the very values that young people hold dear and seemed entirely alien to a generation that felt the benefits of free movement in the EU more than any other. Whether this will hold true or not is yet to be seen.

There is some proof for it in the 2017 general election vote, though. It would hardly be fair to say that Jeremy Corbyn was seen as the 'stop Brexit' candidate. He has been criticised in the British press for more than a year for his 'half-hearted' campaigning during the referendum. His parliamentary party tried to remove him owing to his Euroscepticism. The story of his betrayal of the young was everywhere before the general election. Yet those same people still came to his aid and backed the Labour Party in such great numbers. This suggests a majority of them have accepted the result of the referendum, but just want a better vision for how it will be done. There should be no worry within the Labour Party concerning a conflict between its position on Brexit and its support for the young. I am sure that outriders and those opposed to the Labour leader will continue to use this issue as the basis for an attack. It does not seem to have worked yet and I remain doubtful that it will.

We know that young people are crying out for the opportunity to gain meaningful and secure employment. Unsurprisingly, they want to enjoy their lives and make something of themselves. Unfortunately, our current system does not even allow for this basic aspiration. More people find themselves trapped in insecure work than ever before and young people are disproportionately impacted by the rise of zero-hours contracts. Stagnating wages and collapsing real take-home pay continues to hit the young the hardest. Young members of the BME community find themselves suffering an even worse plight than their white counterparts, with opportunities near nil for over 40 per cent of young black men.

This situation cannot continue. What we need is for the Labour Party to engage with British trade unions to address the current crisis in the workplace. Young people should be encouraged to take their new-found political activism to work. Joining a union, signing up friends and co-workers must be the next step in our revolution. Working with organisers, there is no reason why we could not transform the workplace and ensure decent standards and pay for all. It has been achieved before and it could be achieved again if young people choose to turn up within their trade union branches as they did at the 2017 general election.

Though this is no easy task, it is one that our biggest unions should already be embarking on. Registering the same young people who have become enthused by Corbyn's radical message should be perfectly possible. Establishing specific campaigns to unionise those in the retail and night-time economy sectors would be a good way for the left to show that it was interested in making radical changes to the lives of young people while they remain out of government. Showing them that practical change can be achieved beyond

Westminster would be an effective way of convincing more to vote, so as to ensure that such change could be embedded for all.

We know that 16- and 17-year-olds are also desperate to become actively involved in our democracy. From the anecdotal evidence of them wishing they could vote at the 2017 general election, or the stories of those out campaigning even though they couldn't, to the previous evidence of the engagement of these young people in the Scottish independence referendum, it is clear that there is appetite for lowering the voting age. Capturing this enthusiasm at a young age so that it can continue throughout their lives would be productive for society as a whole.

Sadly, it would not be so productive for the Conservative Party, who, as noted, would be adding another million votes in opposition to themselves, which is a big factor in their decision to oppose it. This could, of course, change. If the Conservative Party were actually to offer something concrete to appeal to young people, that might not be the case at all, and they could regain some of the voters they have lost.

The calls for lowering the voting age must get louder as we head towards the next general election. Though often seen as something of a fringe issue, continuing to deny 16- and 17-year-olds the vote goes against everything modern democracy should be about. We have a duty to renew and refresh our democracy and to keep it relevant – that is what we did when we extended suffrage in the past. It is time to press the refresh button again and welcome 16- and 17-year-olds to their rightful place within our electoral system. Failing to do so will only continue to convince the young that establishment politics remains uninterested in their concerns and their participation.

We know that young voices in Parliament have also played a part alongside – to use a phrase coined by Shadow Chancellor John McDonnell – the older 'greybeards' in encouraging young people to become involved in the democratic process. Whether it be Mhairi Black's clear competence on the Commons floor as a young politician or the new Labour voices that are causing a stir in Westminster, such as Laura Pidcock, Dan Carden and Danielle Rowley among others, it is clear that such figures have a role to play in demonstrating that politics is not the preserve of the old and that it belongs to all of us.

Recapturing the political scene from an older generation will take a lot of time and hard work. But given many senior members are keen to engage young people in the political process, this may be easier to achieve than we think. Corbyn is the prime example of an older politician willing to give a platform to the voice of the young. With many current MPs knowing that the rise in their vote share relies on keeping young people engaged, we may see some attempt to give more attention to the issues that affect our generation. This would be a welcome change to what often seems like distant debate in a chamber that is more often than not filled with braying politicians that act like animals.

Changing the nature of Parliament is an important step in ensuring that politics remains accessible to young people. Now that we know that they are keen to change political discourse, it is up to our current politicians to prove that they are capable of doing this or they will face a challenge from younger candidates who wish to represent the views of our generation.

The mainstream press got their 2017 general election prediction very wrong. One of the reasons they got it so wrong is because most outlets fail to feature young voices within their political coverage. Most of it is informed by conversations held within the Westminster bubble – that is, journalists and politicians talking over coffee or something stronger within the parliamentary estate. It is no wonder that coverage remains so skewed when the establishment media is so concerned with what is happening within this estate rather than within the wider country.

We need our media to embed young voices within the heart of the debate, rather than simply asking 'will young people vote?' when a general election comes around. Some interest in the youth vote has sparked a new engagement between the young and the political system, though this seems largely focused on what the Conservative Party will do to engage them, rather than asking young people themselves what would make them engage with the right. Perhaps the staggering level of support the young continue to invest in the Labour Party renders this question redundant. It is somewhat surprising that the Conservatives have not seriously attempted some sort of consultation with the young people who left them in their droves between the 2015 general election and this most recent contest. If the mainstream media is interested in discovering what caused young Conservative voters to abandon the party in favour of a radical socialist alternative, this would be a useful question to be asking.

We know that the Labour Party did not win the last

election. Despite the hope and the optimism felt throughout the campaign, which was the inspiration for this book,
we did not do enough. That isn't to diminish what was
achieved. All of Labour's senior figures remain frustrated
at the failure to take power at the 2017 general election.
Activists are equally disappointed. But the Conservative
Party also failed to win the election. Their reign is now
dependent on the whims of ten Democratic Unionist Party
members. And with the questions about the Irish border
looming large in the Brexit talks, who knows how secure
that link is?

The real winners of the last election were the young. We
robbed the Conservative Party of their majority and we
prevented Theresa May from introducing domestic legislation that would have hurt our generation as we would have
been sent hurtling back decades into the past. Our collective energy refused her the mandate she craved. Our power
remains within our solidarity and belief that a better future
is possible. We know that we have more to give. We know
that there is hard work to do. But we know that there are
better days to come. We know that we are the future. We
know that we will win.

A GLOBAL REVOLUTION

What is happening with young people in the UK also seems
to be replicating itself across the Western world. It just so
happens that a similar revolution occurred in the United
States. Sadly, for those of us on the left, it didn't happen
during the 2016 presidential election. But it did happen.

Throughout the 2016 presidential primaries and caucuses, Bernie Sanders won more votes from those under the age of thirty than the two major-party presidential candidates combined. CIRCLE analysis of vote tallies estimates that Bernie Sanders won 2,052,081 young votes throughout this process, whereas Donald Trump won 828,675 and Hillary Clinton picked up 766,425.

Some were surprised that after the twenty-one states included in this study had declared, Clinton was behind Donald Trump when it came to young voters. Though Clinton would eventually win more young votes in the election, her lead among the young did not match that which Barack Obama achieved in both of his successful elections. In April 2016, Bernie campaign volunteer Nikhil Goyal wrote in *Time*: 'Sanders supporters like myself are declaring: Our institutions and the political and economic establishment have been royally screwing us over, and we're not going to take it anymore.'

Such a sentiment is exactly what I have been hearing again and again on both sides of the pond. When I was in Chicago during the Democratic Socialists of America 2017 conference, I was pleasantly surprised to see striking similarities between there and what is happening here at home. The left has been revitalised by an injection of enthusiastic young supporters who may yet be the ones to save the world from the forces of far-right politics. It is a bitter irony that young people, ignored by democratic institutions for decades, are now a vital line of defence when it comes to ensuring that such institutions are not devastated by the new populist forces of the right that we see emerging within our politics.

Though there are similarities between the UK and the US, the Democrats seem reluctant to engage with this revolution. Clinton's latest attack on Bernie Sanders in *What Happened* – note the lack of a question mark in the title – demonstrates that the American establishment has failed to learn the lessons of what Sanders started and what Corbyn has confirmed. Sanders' surge shows that young Americans are calling out for a similar political revolution.

In her latest book, *Hacks: The Inside Story of the Break-ins and Breakdowns that Put Donald Trump in the White House*, former Democratic National Committee chair Donna Brazile makes the extraordinary claim that Clinton effectively robbed Sanders of the party's nomination. The feeling that the contest had been rigged against Sanders was a key complaint of many of his supporters.

Interestingly, in a phone conversation between Brazile and Sanders, where she gave her assessment of Clinton's chances of winning the presidential election, she noted her lack of appeal with young people. After Sanders asked Brazile for her assessment of the current position, she notes: 'I had to be frank with him. I did not trust the polls, I said. I told him I had visited states around the country and I found a lack of enthusiasm for her everywhere. I was concerned about the Obama coalition and about millennials.'

But in a sign that it is those on the progressive American left who understand what needs to be done to beat Trump in 2020, Jeffrey Weaver, the campaign chief for Sanders, wasn't bitter. Instead, he argued that the party had to 'open up' to those millennials Brazile feared would not turn out for Clinton: 'Let me tell this to the elites who today still control much of the Democratic Party apparatus: If you do not open up the party, if you do not allow the people in, if you do not advocate for the types of reforms that we need, you will be destroying the opportunity we have to take on Donald Trump.'

So far, the Democratic Party establishment has failed to change course. In its place, the Democratic Socialists of America are on the rise, attempting to capitalise on the failure of the establishment party to galvanise the young support that Sanders managed to earn. Reporting back in February 2017, Jennifer Swann wrote for *Rolling Stone* about the DSA tour that was sweeping local chapters across the United States. Swann noted that Hannah Allison, a 29-year-old organiser with the DSA, was touring the US 'on a mission to get new members – especially younger and more diverse individuals, including those catalysed by Bernie Sanders' campaign – excited about organising toward so-called democratic socialism'.

Just as with Corbyn's campaign in the 2017 general election, much of the activity is being organised by 'a legion of social-media-savvy young followers' who feel 'angry and disillusioned with the Democratic Party in the aftermath of the 2016 presidential election'. The group uses Sanders' student membership of the 'Young People's Socialist League' as evidence of his more radical leanings and potential support for a party that isn't the Democratic one. In truth, they don't need to do so – Sanders was elected to the US Senate as an Independent and has made clear time and again that he plans to continue to do so. Whether he will seek the Democratic nomination for the 2020 election remains a mystery. It certainly seems as if Sanders is still running an active and permanent campaign, but given that he will be seventy-nine by this time it seems more likely that he will use his influence to endorse a younger candidate of the left.

Beyond Sanders, the DSA continues to rise. In an article published by *Vice* in October 2017, writers Alex Thompson and Diamond Naga Siu began their assessment of socialism on American campuses by saying that 'seizing the means of production is so hot right now'. The article accepts that the number of DSA chapters is dwarfed by the 'Democratic Party's College Democrats of America's 1,200 chapters' but notes that 'the sudden surge of an alternative progressive movement among the young threatens to further splinter the Democratic Party as it tries to rebuild after the disastrous 2016 election and energize young voters in 2018 and 2020'.

The point that this new group may 'splinter' the left is one that Sabrina Singh, the deputy communications director for the DNC, disagrees with. Commenting on the rise of the Young Democratic Socialists of America, Singh told *Vice*: 'This is only a good thing for the Democratic Party . . . There is an incredible enthusiasm on college campuses across the country, and we've seen a number of groups rise to bring about progressive change and get involved in Democratic politics.'

The overarching DSA group has mobilised to stand candidates in Democratic primaries against more traditional candidates, and so while the group is also organising in different areas, it is not yet a political party of its own and is instead organising within others. But such work is in contrast to the Democratic Party establishment consensus. In a CNN town hall event, Nancy Pelosi – the House Minority Leader – told young people: 'We're capitalists and that's just the way it is.'

Perhaps that is the reason the DNC remain confused when it comes to targeting Donald Trump. A 2016 Harvard Kennedy School poll from the Institute of Politics titled 'Survey of Young Americans' Attitudes towards Politics and Public Service' found that of those surveyed between the ages of eighteen and twenty, 51 per cent said that they did not support capitalism. A Reason-Rupe poll published in 2015 asked Americans to rate how they felt about capitalism and socialism, with millennials being the only age group where a majority viewed socialism positively, with 53 per cent of those under the age of thirty backing it. Further to this, a Gallup poll in 2015 found that 69 per cent of those aged eighteen to twenty-nine would consider voting for a socialist candidate for president, while only 34 per cent of those aged over sixty-five would.

The fact that these findings appeared before Sanders' campaign only suggests that support for his movement and his platform may just be getting started. When you look at many of the Democratic primary entrance and exit polls, it is easy to see that this might be the case. Figures published by CNN help to demonstrate the support that Sanders received from the young. In Iowa, 84 per cent of the under-30s voted for the Vermont senator compared to just 14 per cent for Hillary Clinton. When narrowed down to even younger primary voters, Sanders won 86 per cent of the under-25s in the same poll. In New Hampshire, the story was much the same, with Sanders securing 83 per cent of the 18–29 vote. In Nevada, the figure was the same. Even in the South – where Clinton recorded her big wins and Sanders' campaign hit something of a roadblock – the Independent senator continued to remain ahead with the young, winning 60 per cent of the 17–24 vote in the South Carolina primary, 61 per cent of the 18–24 vote in Georgia, 62 per cent of the same age bracket in Texas and 66 per cent of the 18–24 vote in Florida.

In the fairly reliable Democratic states that Trump won from Clinton – Wisconsin and Michigan – Sanders secured 84 per cent of the 18–24-year-old vote, 79 per cent of the 25–29-year-old vote and 69 per cent of the 30–39-year-old vote in the first and 85 per cent, 75 per cent and 59 per cent in the same age groups in the second. If the Democratic Party had held these two states, and just one of Ohio, Pennsylvania or Florida, then Donald Trump would not be in the White House. In all three, Sanders was much more popular than Clinton among young voters.

The national exit poll released on the night of the US election suggested that more young people supported a third-party candidate in 2016 than in the previous election. It also revealed that fewer under-30s voted for Clinton than they did for Obama in 2012, with 60 per cent opting for the Democratic Party in 2012 and 55 per cent doing the same in 2016. Republican support held steady at 37 per cent, while the third-party candidate increased from 3 per cent to 8 per cent. It is worth considering what could have happened in Michigan had Clinton been able to achieve just a few more percentage points with young voters in a state that Trump won by just over 10,000 votes, or 0.23 per cent.

The day after the election, Bloomberg ran an article on young voters with the sub-heading: 'Had only millennials voted, Clinton would've won in a landslide'. It is important to read the headline carefully, as what Bloomberg is suggesting is that had 18–29-year-olds been the only American citizens able to vote, Clinton would have won 473 electoral college votes to Trump's 32 (in the actual election, Trump won 306 to Clinton's 232). What the article does note, however, is that the Democrats failed to win over enough young white voters. According to the exit poll analysis conducted by the Centre for Information & Research on Civic Learning and Engagement, young white voters opted for Trump over Clinton by 48 per cent to 43 per cent. Though hardly a crushing victory, it is concerning that young white voters were more likely to support the Republican Party than they were the Democrats. As Bloomberg notes, however, there is little time for Republican fanfare over this fact given that 'the election had the fourth-lowest turnout by young voters for a GOP nominee since 1972'. On the night of the election, political commentator Van Jones emotionally gave his verdict of Trump's victory:

> People have talked about a miracle, I'm hearing about a nightmare. It is hard to be a parent tonight for a lot of us. You tell your kids, don't be a bully. You tell your kids, don't be a bigot. You tell your kids, do your homework and be prepared. Then you have this outcome . . . This was many things. This was a rebellion against the elites, true. It was a complete reinvention of politics and polls. But it was also something else . . . This was a whitelash, a whitelash against a changing country, a whitelash against a black president in part.

Jones' words seem particularly poignant given that young white people apparently opted for Trump over Clinton. Given that Trump's disapproval rating among young people now consistently stands at over 60 per cent in a number of polls, it seems hard to believe that so many young white people came out to vote for him.

In my opinion, there is a link here to the disaffected vote. Whereas in the 2017 UK general election, young people from across the country could vent their disaffection in an outsider, young people in America did not have quite that choice. Yes, Trump is a monster. Yes, his political ideology (which, let's be frank, isn't entirely obvious) is scary. But Trump was the change candidate in the election. Trump told young, white working-class people that he was going to make their country great again. He did so at a time when Clinton was speaking about how great America already was at rallies across the country. What she was missing was the fact that for many young people, America isn't great.

Friends that I have in the US are ashamed of their government's continuous refusal to do anything about the gun lobby, considering the regular and horrific mass shootings. Young Americans working three jobs just to get by don't believe that America is great. Progressive young Americans are ashamed of the fact that Obama deported more people than any other president. It is no wonder that more young people opted for a third-party candidate than before. We also should not be surprised that young, white working-class people split fairly evenly between Trump and Clinton, given the way the liberal establishment that Clinton defends, and of which she had been such a central part, has treated them over the past few decades.

Whereas Clinton's response to Trump's call of 'Make America Great Again' was some version of 'we already are great!', Sanders spoke specifically to the young. In an opinion piece for *Vice Impact*, he argued:

Making America great is not spending tens of billions more on weapons systems or providing trillions in tax breaks for the very rich. Rather, it is having a well-educated population that can compete in the global economy, and making it possible that every American, regardless of income, has the opportunity to get the education they need to thrive.

Sanders congratulated Trump for successfully tapping into what he called the 'anger of a declining middle class that is sick and tired of establishment economics, establishment politics and the establishment media'. It was a message that resonated with the young, with Sanders eclipsing Obama's 2008 primary youth vote record before the primaries even ended. In this sense, young people were clearly flocking to a message that hit the elites hardest. It was a message that Clinton found impossible to deliver, given her own links to establishment figures in the worlds of economics, politics and the media.

If the Democratic Party is to reap the support of the young, it must quickly learn the lessons of Corbyn's 2017 campaign and place them at the centre of its future. A failure to do so will only let down every single American citizen – as well as those of us across the world – who depend on ensuring that Trump loses the presidency in 2020.

Across Europe the picture is a different and darker one. We have yet to see Labour's left-wing sister parties embrace a Corbynite message that young people can become engaged with. In 2017, the left did poorly in the Netherlands, France and Germany. Speaking at the Europe Together conference of centre-left parties in Brussels, Corbyn was welcomed with standing ovations as the 'new Prime Minister of Britain'. Some socialist comrades in the hall even chanted: 'Oh, Jeremy Corbyn'.

Despite the fanfare, it was Corbyn's message that Europe's left must follow that stood out. Corbyn noted that 'for too long the most prominent voices in our movement have looked out of touch, too willing to defend the status quo and the established order' owing to 'a desperate attempt to protect what is seen as the centre ground of politics: only to find the centre ground has shifted or was never where the elites thought it was in the first place'.

In 2014, many were excited by the rise of Podemos in Spain and Syriza in Greece. Podemos largely grew out of huge street demonstrations powered by young people and Syriza appeared as a response to mass unemployment in Greece. Like Labour in 2017, Podemos was labelled as a 'radical' and 'Marxist' party, but information released in 2015 from the CIS – the sociological research institute – demonstrated that young people were behind the surge. In the last round of Spanish elections, young people opted for the left-wing coalition Unidos Podemos more than any other party, while the over-65s stood firm with the ruling conservative Partido Popular.

In Spain, the problems facing young people are much the same as those we face here in the UK. The position that young people in the UK find themselves in is replicated across the globe, and though youth surges may not have happened everywhere yet, there is no reason why they cannot or will not. In many ways, this book serves as a guide as to how such a surge can be achieved across Europe and the wider world. The attitude taken by Jeremy Corbyn and Labour's policy platform is perfectly achievable in other nations – in fact, some of it has already been achieved elsewhere – if left-wing parties are willing to engage with the new socialism. Young people across the European states seem to remain locked in the view that their politics does nothing for them. Corbyn is right to argue, then, that his comrades should follow his lead. Making politics work for young people is exactly what ensured our involvement in the first place and this is something that can be done should politicians take the time and the interest to do so.

UpRising

The rise of young people corresponds with the growth of new, engaging and unashamedly left-wing ideas. Though some have marked Jeremy Corbyn's platform as a return to a bygone era, the truth is that socialism is being reformed alongside this new engagement of the young. The 2008 financial crisis sparked the need to revisit the fundamental nature of our society and our economy, but it has taken nearly ten years for the Labour Party and the wider labour movement to properly assess what we must do next.

Now, reinvigorated by the participation of the young, it is clear that the left has an answer as to where we go next. The stranglehold of neoliberalism – or, simply, the favouring of the will of free markets – is loosening across our country. Left-wing activists and campaigners have been talking about the flaws of the ideology for decades, indeed, since its inception. But it is only recently that such voices have been accompanied by unlikely allies. Take, for example, the IMF – long criticised by the left for its neoliberal policies – who in 2016 questioned 'aspects of the neoliberal agenda that have not delivered as expected'. In October 2017, the institution went a step further, using its half-yearly fiscal reporting to rally behind the key argument of Corbynomics: that economic growth would not suffer if we forced the top 5 per cent of earners to pay a higher rate of tax. Though Theresa May attacks Labour for living on 'planet Venezuela', she also admitted at the Conservative Party conference that 'we thought there was a political consensus . . . Jeremy Corbyn changed that'.

It does not really matter if May's premiership survives all that long, given that it is the ideology underpinning the Conservative government that finds itself slipping away into irrelevance at the same pace as their own grasp on power. In April 2016, George Monbiot noted in a *Guardian* column that neoliberalism had played its part in almost every disaster we continue to witness, whether it be the financial crash, the continued degradation of our planet or the political crisis which sees Donald Trump elected leader of the free world. At the end of his column, he argued: 'A coherent alternative has to be proposed. For Labour, the Democrats and the wider left, the central task should be to develop an economic Apollo programme, a conscious attempt to design a new system, tailored to the demands of the twenty-first century.'

He is right. But this is what is happening in Britain today. Yes, much of the economic philosophy of the left remains rooted in Keynesian thought, but the introduction of young voices has led to the creation of this new and fluid socialism, whereby the ideology is being redrafted and reorganised for the modern world. Much of what is being developed is in opposition to neoliberalism, but as we have seen in the 2017 general election, much of it is also based on what people want, as opposed to what they don't want.

There will always be debate over how neoliberalism is defined, but what is undeniable is that the ideology places the interests of capital above the interests or welfare of people. In particular, it places the interests of capital well above the welfare of young people. Though Tory austerity has led to an overall reduction in public spending as a share of the whole economy, it has mainly hit the young. Unison estimates that some 600 youth centres have been closed since 2010 and 3,500 youth work positions have also been lost. Hundreds of millions of pounds have been slashed on budgets that exist to serve young people.

At the 2017 general election, Corbyn did not just present an alternative to the Conservative Party, but an alternative to the entire foundation upon which our politics is based. We have seen Margaret Thatcher's slogan of 'there is no alternative' ripped up and replaced with a positive vision for the future. Until now, no mainstream party has challenged the neoliberal consensus in the way that Corbyn's Labour

Party has. I believe that much of the discontent concerning neoliberalism reared its head during the European referendum, particularly with disaffected voters and the young. The 'Remain' campaign failed to understand that it was implicitly supporting a neoliberal consensus that many were turning to reject. The 'Leave' campaign was able to take such discontent and aim the blame in all the wrong places. Young people found themselves caught in the middle of a campaign that was irrelevant to them – hence why turnout was so low in comparison to the 2017 general election and why so many opted for the safer, more progressive option.

The events organised by the World Transformed alongside the Labour Party conference in Brighton 2017 and Liverpool 2016 will stand as a testament to the new socialism in action. It was at these sessions that real people were able to participate and engage with policy in a way that we had not seen before – many of them young people wanting to become involved for the first time. Whether they knew it or not, the young people speaking out at these events were speaking out against the neoliberal consensus and it is the ideology that they turned out to vote against in the 2017 general election.

But we should not just credit the turnout to a rejection of neoliberal ideas. Young people also decided to become involved because they felt like they were part of something much bigger than themselves. For the first time in many years, campaigning for the Labour Party felt as if you were doing so on behalf of a real movement. There was a genuine feeling that this was not just about us, but that it was about all of society and, importantly, the future of that society. The new socialism that continues to be generated by the engagement of the young is not so much an accord written on paper, but a participatory project that continues to evolve as more people get involved and present innovative solutions to the problems that we face.

The social and political revolution that has been brought about by Jeremy Corbyn's rise and the participation of the young is unlike anything we have seen since the 1980s. The number of people attending Corbyn's rallies, and the passion and enthusiasm contained within such events, is a return to what went on then.

For example, looking back to October 1981, it is possible to see how much of this energy found its place in the Campaign for Nuclear Disarmament (CND). The so-called 'Second Wave' saw the campaign group amass 90,000 national members and over 250,000 in local branches. That month, 250,000 joined the CND march in London and the demonstration against the Cruise missile deployment in October 1983 saw roughly 300,000 people demonstrating in the capital in solidarity with millions across Europe.

Student CND and Youth CND were active campaign groups with thousands of members. Young people found a home within the radical call for a different way of doing international politics and a different way of practising diplomacy at the height of the Cold War. The Labour Party adopted the policy of unilateral disarmament at its 1982 conference before being crushed in the 1983 general election.

A year later, the miners' strike also spurred people into action. The fight between Thatcher and the unions encapsulated a real fight between two entirely different ideologies.

But after the defeat of the National Union of Mineworkers (NUM) and the disgraceful response of the Conservative Party, the political argument appeared to have been won by the forces of the right. Rather than attempting to change the world, many sunk into the belief that they must find a way to live within it and do well from it.

Activism obviously did not disappear entirely, however, and political rivalry would soon find itself reaffirmed in the poll tax riots at the end of the 1980s. But from here on out, with Labour's loss in the 1992 general election, our political discourse became somewhat united. Labour policy nearly mirrored Conservative policy, as John Major, John Smith and Tony Blair were all less confrontational figures drawn to the centre ground and consensus.

Again, rather than changing the world, the mainstream of the party appeared content to work with it. Despite huge majorities and an overwhelming electoral endorsement, successive Blair governments failed to implement the more radical elements of Labour's left. Yes, we have the minimum wage, we banned fox hunting and we brought our public services back from the brink. Nobody of sane mind denies that New Labour did some good, but it had the opportunity to do much more. But then how much of a socialist agenda could realistically have been achieved under a Labour prime minister who was fairly open in his admiration for Thatcher?

For a generation, our politics became less polarised and a cushy consensus formed around Westminster, to the point where in 2017 the suggestion by a Labour MP that she does not want to drink with Conservative members on the parliamentary terrace is held as a disgraceful and unacceptable comment. But it is a polarised politics that people have been calling for, whether they know it or not. Behind every utterance of 'all politicians are the same' rests the consensus that we have allowed to blossom within our politics. Corbyn's election as Labour leader, the 2017 general election result and the rise of the young are factors that have occurred as a result of frustration with the current system and a desire for it to be fundamentally altered.

Young people sent a shockwave through the political system and stuck two fingers up at a political elite that has been too confident in ignoring their concerns. Assured by the terrifyingly low turnout figures of the young over the past few decades, we know that politicians of all stripes felt as though they could ignore the young to keep their older voters sweet. To protect elderly benefits in the UK – such as winter fuel payments for pensioners and free bus travel for the over-65s – young people had their university tuition fees trebled and students from disadvantaged backgrounds had maintenance grants transferred into loans, forcing them into more debt at the beginning of their lives. Such an imbalance was protected by the fact that young people failed to show up on election day. But that's not going to happen anymore. Politicians who were reliant on suppressing the young vote now find themselves in a dangerous position.

Though the idea that Corbyn's politics will take us back in time is used as political rhetoric, there is some basis to it. As William Davies noted in the *London Review of Books*, Corbyn's ability to cast a critical look at the not-so-distant past stands as a testament to how we may be able to develop a different future across the globe:

Reacting to the breakdown of the vote on 8 June, business leaders and conservative commentators have expressed their disquiet at the fact that young people are so enthusiastic about an apparently retrograde left-wing programme. 'Memo to anyone under 45,' Digby Jones, the former director general of the CBI, tweeted: 'You can't remember last time socialists got control of the cookie jar: everything nationalised & nothing worked.' To which the rebuke might be made: and you don't remember how good things were compared to today. Speak to my undergraduate students (many of them born during Blair's first term) about the 1970s and early 1980s, and you'll see the wistful look on their faces as they imagine a society in which artists, writers and recent graduates could live independently in Central London, unharassed by student loan companies, workfare contractors or debt collectors. This may be a partial historical view, but it responds to what younger generations are currently cheated of: the opportunity to grow into adulthood without having their entire future mapped out as a financial strategy. A leader who can build a bridge to that past offers the hope of a different future.

It is right to argue that everything has changed, but the obsession with the idea that change is always good has clearly failed to materialise. For young people, life has got worse. So when we are attacked for supporting an old man from the 'past', some of us can grasp what it is that Davies touches on. Being able to live is important, and it is so distressing that owing to the failings of capital and to right-wing ideology young people are not even able to live their lives. We are now beyond cogs in a machine. In this context, turning back the clock seems like a nice idea.

But great change can happen and I am not so pessimistic as to believe that young people should be forced to accept what our generation once had in the past. Indeed, with the growth of technology, we should be demanding more than ever. In the 2017 general election, we certainly demanded more than we have before and achieved more than we have before, but there is still a new world to be won. I believe that it can only be won by looking forward and continuing the recent rise that we have all witnessed, not just in the next UK general election, but across the globe. The revolution of the young can and should be fostered in every community and in every country.

Young people from across the world need to stand in solidarity with one another in demanding that the current settlement we have been offered is nowhere near good enough. But it remains up to the left, and those who have influence within it, to ensure that they are doing all they can to engage and to enthuse young voices so that they can believe and trust in the political system once again. This starts by following the model that has been analysed within this book: namely what Jeremy Corbyn has done since 2015.

The first thing that the left must do is open themselves up. This will be difficult for some because it will require a period of serious self-reflection, where party establishments must ask themselves the following pertinent questions: Why are young people rejecting us? What did we do in power to push young people away? How can we change this? The third question is perhaps the most important. But it is a question that should also be directed outwards. Just as Corbyn and the Labour Party asked young people what was wrong and how they could help, the left must show that it is willing to listen. I cannot stress enough how important this seemingly slight point is. Young people do not want to be spoken to or shouted at; we are far too used to that sort of politics and any attempt at reforming relationships with this strategy will only stain a party with the stench of the old politics. For young people to engage with politics, politics must first engage with them. Those in power now will only continue to deepen the crisis that young people find themselves in if they follow their own historic record.

This is why it is so important that next time around, whether in the United States or in Spain, that the left has realised these lessons. It will not be enough for anybody – particularly those in the Labour Party here at home – to turn around after the next round of elections in any given state and ask 'where were the young people?' if they themselves have failed to actively engage with my generation. Though I remain confident that young people will maintain their passion here in the UK, I am deeply concerned by what is happening in the United States. It is so important that young people find a home within the Democratic Party if the forces of progress are to win at the next election and remove Donald Trump from office. What the Democratic Party is failing to do is to heed the warning that Corbyn gave to his European comrades, with establishment figures on the left in the US seemingly more worried about themselves and their own position than the damaging potential of second Trump term.

Young people can stop this happening at the next election, but they cannot be blamed if they do not, owing to a complete lack of engagement from a party establishment that fails to learn what Sanders taught them in 2016. Given that the lessons are there to be learned and that Labour's 2017 general election campaign serves as a blueprint of how to 'do' youth engagement properly, there can be no excuses for anyone that fails to capitalise on the fact that young people are crying out for change.

It is important that we understand exactly what has happened here. It isn't just that young people have become engaged and have been enthused by Corbyn's radical message. It isn't just that neoliberalism is seemingly collapsing around us. It isn't just that the political consensus has been torn apart. What has happened is a seismic shift in the way that politics is done. In many ways, politics itself has been irreversibly changed into something that is much more reflective of society than it has been before.

Corbyn defied the traditional idea that the mainstream media controlled messaging and thus national opinion, and he defied the idea that young people and 'non-voters' would not come out. But he also made politics more human. For the first time in a very long time, politics felt like a tangible concept that people could connect with. Politics has been changed for ever by a left-wing leader willing to break all the rules, supported by a movement of young people that refused to believe politics must remain the same. The hope that has been entrusted within the left in the UK can find its place in any left-wing movement that is willing to do what has been suggested here. Though there is a real need for Corbyn to maintain his support among the young, it is in all our interest that his message and his vision becomes the foundation upon which others learn how to engage.

Yes, young people must also accept that they have a role to play in showing up and getting involved. But we have seen this happen in the UK from the point at which it seemed like politics could change, the moment Corbyn announced his intention to run for the Labour Party leadership. They didn't need to be promised the earth to get involved, they just needed to know that there was a genuine chance of transforming politics for the better. This point is perhaps the simplest way of explaining the potential that exists within this movement. Together, young people and passionate politicians that are genuinely interested in radically changing the current settlement can change everything. In the undying words of Karl Marx, we have a world to win. We owe it to all those who came before us, and the young people who will come after, to bloody get on and win it.

Afterword

Getting Involved

If we are going to continue to build this movement, the most important thing that anybody can do – or that you can urge anybody to do – is to ensure that they are registered to vote at: gov.uk/register-to-vote. As I have argued, it is a crying shame that registration is not automatic and that anybody should have to 'claim' their vote. But this is the system we are operating in and it is more important than ever that we take the time to check whether we are properly registered as well as urging others to do the same.

For change to happen in the Labour Party, you must be part of it. Jeremy Corbyn is living proof of that very message. So the next important step is to make sure that you are a member of the Labour Party. You can join at: join. labour.org.uk. When you do, keep the hope, the optimism and the enthusiasm of the 2017 general election campaign alive. Attend your local constituency meetings, organise in your local areas. With a surging youth membership there is nothing that we cannot achieve.

I'd also suggest that you join Momentum. Joining this group allows you the opportunity to fight back online and to also meet with like-minded people in your local CLP. You can join at: join.peoplesmomentum.com.

Aside from party politics, there are two organisations that I would recommend joining and then work on reforming. The first is the UK Youth Parliament (ukyouthparliament. org.uk) and the second is the British Youth Council (byc. org.uk). I am happy to advocate these organisations for the brilliant work they do in giving young people the confidence to have a voice. But as I have touched on, these organisations need the energy and passion of the 2017 general election to be pumped into them. You can do that by joining up and getting involved.

There are then numerous other organisations that I personally support and would want young people to offer their time to. Joining these campaign groups allows you to 'specialise' your interests and campaigning. The Youth section of the Campaign for Nuclear Disarmament is an important pressure group that needs support now, as young people rally to the political cause (yscnd.org). The same goes for the League Against Cruel Sports, which offers a youth membership to all those concerned about animal welfare and animal rights (league.org.uk/donate/youth-membership-under-16). Youth organisations exist for almost every campaign group, so a search for any issue you care about should return an organisation. If not, then start one up.

ACKNOWLEDGEMENTS

This book would not have been possible without the guidance, support and belief of my agent, Natalie Galustian. At a time when few believed in what I was saying, Natalie engaged and remained interested in what I was writing. She has become a great friend of mine and I will remain eternally grateful for all that she has done to make this happen. Natalie has gone above and beyond what would be expected of a literary agent, helping to ensure that my writing was as sharp as it could be. She is an absolute star and anybody would be lucky to have her represent them half as well as she has represented me.

Secondly, I want to thank my publisher, and particularly my editor, Ian Marshall. I am so grateful for the help and support that he has offered throughout this process. Ian has tempered me where necessary, as well as ensuring that my passion and conviction are not lost within my writing. He has been a tremendous support, without which this book would not have come to be published. I would also like to record my thanks to the wider team at Simon & Schuster, particularly Amy Fulwood and Helen Upton, for all that they have done.

I want to acknowledge the love and support that has always been shown to me by my family, who have served to ensure that I kept on track at all times. My mum, Rachael, and my grandparents, Roland and Linda, have been – and always will be – the rocks upon which all of this is built. I would also like to acknowledge my sisters, Demi, Marie and Carly, and my dad, Carl, despite his less than favourable view of politics. Further thanks go to my Merlot-drinking partner and step-father, Mark. A special vote of thanks goes to Tracy Sanders, my English literature teacher, for sparking the whole damn thing.

The final acknowledgement must go to all of the young people who contributed to making this happen, including the hundreds who emailed me with written submissions to some of the questions that I needed answering. I set out with the mission of ensuring that this book was not just about me or my opinions, but the wider movement. I hope that I have done these people proud.